THROUGH
UNEXPLORED
TEXAS

Notes taken during the expedition
commanded by Capt. R. B. Marcy, U.S.A.,

THROUGH
UNEXPLORED
TEXAS

*in the summer and fall
of 1854*

By W. B. Parker
Attached to the Expedition

Introduction by
George B. Ward

The Texas State Historical Association

© 1990 Texas State Historical Association, Austin,Texas.
All rights reserved. Printed in the United States of America.

Library of Congress Catalog Card Number: 84-80800

ISBN 0-87611-064-2 Hardback Edition
ISBN 0-87611-065-0 Paperback Edition

10 9 8 7 6 5 4 3 2

Published by The Texas State Historical Association
in Cooperation with the Center for Studies in
Texas History, The University of Texas at Austin

Mr. Clifton Caldwell provided the copy of *Notes taken during the
expedition of Capt. R. B. Marcy, U.S.A., through unexplored Texas, in the
summer and fall of 1854* used to reprint this edition.

Cover: detail of "View Near Head of Red-River" from *Exploration of the
Red River of Louisiana, in the Year 1852,* by Randolph B. Marcy. Cover
design by David Timmons.

The paper used in this book meets the minimum requirements of the
American National Standard for Permanence of Paper for Printed
Library Materials, Z39.48—1984

IN THE INSTANT WORLD in which we live
I often reflect on how many mistakes might
be avoided if we would but listen to
the lessons which history has to teach us.

F RED H. M OORE

The Fred H. and Ella Mae Moore
Texas History Reprint Series

The Texas Revolution
By William C. Binkley

**Spanish Explorers in the
Southern United States, 1528–1543**
Edited by Frederick W. Hodge and
Theodore H. Lewis

A Ranchman's Recollections
By Frank S. Hastings
With a new introduction by
David J. Murrah

**A Comprehensive History of Texas,
1685–1897**
By Dudley Goodall Wooten

Texas
By Mary Austin Holley
With a new introduction by
Marilyn McAdams Sibley

**Report on the United States and
Mexican Boundary Survey**
By Major William H. Emory
With a new introduction by
William H. Goetzmann

The History of Texas
By David B. Edward
With a new introduction by
Margaret S. Henson

*The publication of this series is made possible
by a gift from Fred H. and Ella Mae Moore and
the Mobil Foundation, Inc.*

INTRODUCTION

W. B. Parker's *Notes Taken During the Expedition Commanded by Capt. R. B. Marcy, U.S.A., Through Unexplored Texas, In the Summer and Fall of 1854* is a forgotten book about a largely forgotten man: Randolph Barnes Marcy. The book has been out of print since it was published 128 years ago, and the passage of time has seen the once well-known Marcy fade from public view like a photograph left in the sun. Neither book nor man should be forgotten. *Through Unexplored Texas* is a lively and valuable narrative of frontier exploration that reminds us of the extreme importance of Marcy, and military men like him, in the exploration and development of the American West. Parker's narrative draws a fascinating picture of frontier Texas and reacquaints us with this remarkable army officer who had such a significant influence on the frontier development of the Lone Star State.

Randolph Barnes Marcy was born on April 9, 1812, at Greenwich, Massachusetts. His half-century military career began when he graduated from the United States Military Academy in 1832. He saw limited battlefield action in the war with Mexico, the Second Seminole War, and the Civil War, and he was pro-

claimed "the hero of the Mormon War" for his courageous 634-mile march through the snowbound Rocky
Mountains to get remounts and provisions for the be-
leaguered United States Army. During the Civil War
he was chief-of-staff to his son-in-law, General George
B. McClellan. Marcy's importance is not found on the
battlefield, however, but in his frontier explorations,
which began in 1849. Despite chronic illness, unfairly
low rank and pay, and the difficulties of raising a
family under frontier conditions, Marcy became one
of the important soldier-explorers of his century. Although often frustrated in his career, he could never
resist requesting to lead one more expedition into
unexplored territory. When he retired from the military as a brigadier general in 1881, few men had explored more unknown country, and few men had
provided so much valuable information about the
frontier in their maps and writings.

The purpose of Marcy's 1854 expedition through
unexplored Texas was to locate and survey eighteen
square leagues of wilderness for Indian reservations,
as well as to meet with Texas's nomadic Indians and
convince them to settle on these reserves as farmers.
The Texas legislature instigated the expedition when
it approved an act that offered to donate these lands
for reserves if the United States government would
sponsor an expedition to locate and establish them. In
April of 1854, Adjutant General Samuel Cooper issued orders for Captain Marcy to go to Fort Smith,

Arkansas, and organize an expedition to carry out this act.

Marcy was clearly the man to lead such an expedition. He had been active in Texas since 1845, when he was involved in two early battles of the Mexican War. In 1849 he escorted gold-rush emigrants from Fort Smith to Santa Fe across Texas's forbidding Llano Estacado. The return route that he pioneered across Texas—from Doña Ana, New Mexico, near El Paso, to Fort Smith, Arkansas—marked the establishment of a significant, southern, transcontinental trail. Marcy explored and charted the Brazos River in 1851 and, in the following year, he led his famous expedition to the undiscovered sources of the Red River.

Merely listing Marcy's major exploring expeditions misses a good deal of their importance. Like Lewis and Clark, John C. Frémont, and other celebrated explorers before him, Marcy was much more than a pathfinder with a one-dimensional mission. He was an official agent of the federal government, which had a complex network of political, scientific, military, and economic objectives behind every frontier expedition that it sponsored. Since 1849, Marcy's expeditions had involved a broad range of tasks: exploring the country's geography; examining the land's resources and potential for development; surveying roads and locating new trails; studying, pacifying, and determining the strength of the Plains Indians; noting suitable camping places for travelers and potential sites for military camps and forts; collecting plant and animal life for scientific study; and accurately measuring and mapping the land. Marcy's official report and Parker's narrative of the 1854 expedition make clear that the explorers indeed accomplished many things in addition to locating reservation lands. They carefully explored the unknown areas at the headwaters of the Wichita and Brazos rivers, mapping the topography and collecting soil, minerals, fossils, animals, and vegetation. They appraised the land's potential for farming, ranching, and mining, and they carefully observed many Indians in councils and in chance meetings. They brought not one but a variety of perspectives to bear on the landscape. In pursuing and achieving these objectives, Marcy's 1854 expedition was not unique. He was only one of many men leading such multi-purpose expeditions. Captain Marcy happened, however, to be more active, successful, and influential than most explorers of his generation.

Marcy's accomplishments as a professional explorer are matched by very few military men of the nineteenth century. Unquestionably, the shape of the Texas frontier was molded by Marcy. He built and commanded a number of forts in the Southwest. His 1849 Santa Fe expedition established a major southern route across Texas. When the War Department decided to construct a line of forts across Texas from the Red River to El Paso, they were placed along Marcy's 1849 return route and were built at sites he had

suggested. He was one of the important map-makers
of his generation; the maps he based on his explorations showed for the first time the correct courses of
the Colorado, Brazos, Pecos, and Canadian rivers. His
1852 expedition to the headwaters of the Red River,
accompanied by his future son-in-law, George B. Mc-
Clellan, was the first Anglo-American expedition to
explore and accurately map this important river and
the Palo Duro Canyon. Thomas Freeman and Thomas
Sparks, Zebulon M. Pike, Stephen H. Long, and other
explorers had all tried and failed to locate and map
accurately the entire Red River. Marcy's many official
expedition reports, and the three popular travel books
he wrote based on his career as an explorer, are
among the best primary sources on the nineteenth-
century frontier—its geography, geology, Indian eth-
nology, and plant and animal life. He was simply
one of the best informed and most engaging writers
about the pre–Civil War frontier experience. Marcy
traded ideas on this experience with major scholarly,
scientific, military, and frontier figures of his time,
George Bancroft, Spencer F. Baird, Robert E. Lee,
and Kit Carson among them. The extensive publicity
generated by Marcy's remarkable exploring feats
created awareness of and gave impetus to western development. Although Marcy's name is today largely
unknown—it graces only a Texas ghost town—he put
many names on the land in his years of exploration.

In 1856, New York City businessman and editor

William Brown Parker published *Through Unexplored Texas,* his personal account of the 1854 expedition led by his friend Marcy, who had invited him
to accompany the expedition. It had been Parker's
long-time dream to tour the frontier Southwest. Parker's vision in *Through Unexplored Texas* is filtered
through a decidedly romantic lens. His view of nature, wilderness, and frontier adventure is typical of
the mid-nineteenth-century romantic mind-set; his
vocabulary is dotted with its emotional language. He
describes a river in conventional romantic terms as a
"wild and picturesque scene"; a wilderness thunder-
storm creates for him "a striking picture of the sublime." But what makes Parker's narrative so interesting and valuable is the complexity of his vision. He
portrays the Southwest's beauty in romantic terms but
balances his romantic impressions with realistic and
scientific descriptions. Following a march through the
barren Wichita River country, Parker describes in
close detail how the explorers endured an agonizing
search for water, with the temperature over 110 degrees, only to find a small pocket of rainwater filled
with green scum and snakes.

Parker's images of the Indians they encountered
often depend on familiar stereotypes, both positive
and negative. An attractive female Indian is described
as a "prairie flower"; Indians whom he found less
appealing are portrayed as cruel, degenerate savages.
But Parker sometimes transcends conventional de-

scriptions to take note of complexities. The wealth of ethnographic detail and the rich individual portraits of Indians make *Through Unexplored Texas* a useful resource as well as a revealing reflection of contemporary values. Although Parker faults Indians for what he sees as their fatal flaws, he also notes the responsibility of white men for some of the Indians' problems and asserts that they have a Christian duty to atone for their sins against the Indian. Moreover, when Parker meets Indians whom he admires, or notes their favorable qualities, he is quick to acknowledge them. Parker doubts that the Indians will adopt the white man's ways, but he notes with approval that this expedition to establish the first Plains Indian reservations picked desirable lands with fine water and timber.

Parker's detailed descriptions lend a great deal of color, and historical and anthropological significance, to *Through Unexplored Texas*. His descriptions of cowboys on an early Texas cattle drive, the geography of the Cross Timbers, or the peculiar vocabulary and dialects of frontiersmen, are the kind of details and anecdotes so often missing in more formal reports. Parker does not hesitate to defy the reader's black and white expectations in favor of the many shades of grey that make up the sometimes unpredictable Texas frontier experience.

Parker's narrative runs from the comic to the tragic, the ridiculous to the sublime. He describes the expedition's July Fourth visit to the tiny frontier settlement of Gainesville, Texas, a "one-legged settlement" that literally had four one-legged citizens. Parker cajoled three of them into racing each other for a bottle of whiskey, which resulted in their six crutches and three legs frantically stumping across the Texas prairie in the moonlight. In contrast, the next evening the expedition began a night march into the setting sun that was going down over the distant, unexplored headwaters of the Brazos and Wichita rivers. Parker describes the explorers standing awestruck in the wilderness between a thunderstorm and a prairie fire. He uses striking Biblical imagery to suggest their emotions on being surrounded by a pillar of fire and a pillar of cloud, with the wilderness in between. The reader can feel Parker's fear, awe, and delight as the wildfire reddened the darkening sky and powerful flashes of lightning played off the clouds towering above the wilderness. As in so many other parts of Parker's remarkable narrative, this juxtaposition of violence and beauty captures the contradictions and complexities of the southwestern frontier and the men who explored it when it was truly unknown.

GEORGE B. WARD

NOTES TAKEN

DURING THE EXPEDITION

COMMANDED BY CAPT. R. B. MARCY, U. S. A.,

THROUGH

UNEXPLORED TEXAS,

In the Summer and Fall of 1854.

———◆———

BY W. B. PARKER,

Attached to the Expedition.

———◆———

PHILADELPHIA:

HAYES & ZELL, No. 193 MARKET STREET.

1 8 5 6.

KING & BAIRD, PRINTERS, SANSOM ST.

TO

M Y   W I F E

I Dedicate my Book.

CONTENTS.

———◆———

CHAPTER I.

OBJECT OF THE EXPEDITION.

Act of Texas Legislature.—Capt. Marcy ordered to take Command.—Departure from New York.—Arrival at Fort Smith.—Fitting out the Train.—Departure for Fort Washita.—Incidents of the first two days....................

CHAPTER II.

CHOCTAW AGENCY TO GAINES' CREEK.

CHAPTER III.

GAINES' CREEK TO FORT WASHITA.

Horse bitten by a snake.—Prairie flowers.—Oats met with.—White men married to squaws.—Law upon the subject.—Fossils found.—Coal abund-

CONTENTS.

CHAPTER IV.

STAY AT FORT WASHITA.

CHAPTER V.

FORT WASHITA TO LOWER CROSS TIMBERS.

CHAPTER VI.

LOWER CROSS TIMBERS TO UPPER CROSS TIMBERS.

CONTENTS.

CHAPTER VII.

UPPER CROSS TIMBERS TO LITTLE WITCHITA.

CHAPTER VIII.

LITTLE WITCHITA TO COTTON WOOD SPRING.

CHAPTER IX.

CAMP AT THE COTTON WOOD SPRING.

CHAPTER X.

COTTON WOOD SPRING TO DIVIDING RIDGE.

CHAPTER XI.

DIVIDING RIDGE TO THE HEAD OF THE BRAZOS.

CONTENTS.

CHAPTER XII.

HEAD OF THE BRAZOS TO FLAT ROCK CREEK.

CHAPTER XIII.

FLAT ROCK CREEK TO CLEAR FORK OF THE BRAZOS.

CHAPTER XIV.

CAMP ON CLEAR FORK OF THE BRAZOS.

CONTENTS.

CHAPTER XV.

CAMP ON THE CLEAR FORK TO CAMP ON THE LOWER BRAZOS.

CHAPTER XVI.

THE INDIANS OF THE COUNTRY.

PREFACE.

THESE desultory Notes, taken merely to refresh my memory when recurring to scenes so fraught, to me, with interesting reminiscences, would never have met the public eye had it not been for the kind and flattering solicitations of friends who have perused my journal; and if, by putting them in print, I can excite one-half the interest and pleasure with the general reader which the expedition gave me, I shall be amply repaid for the time spent and the care taken in writing my book.

In the arrangement of my work my object is twofold, viz., to *impart all the information* I can respecting the physical character of the country passed through on the whole line of our march from the frontier, and to *entertain*, by relating from personal observation, scenes and incidents of daily occurrence, whilst roaming through so wild a region as the far South-West.

Associated as I was with men of long experience in the performance of similar duties, my observations have been aided by scientific knowledge, whilst the protection of a government escort gave opportunity for close inspection, without the harrassing anticipation of attack and disaster—a great barrier to thorough investigation of a country by private parties.

PREFACE.

Many of my scenes and incidents in prairie and Indian life are a personal narrative. Where not, they are taken from the mouths of those who were witnesses or actors in them, and whose long experience gives them a right to full confidence on my part.

As a personal narrative, I have not thought proper to be minute, but in mentioning soil, climate and natural history have spoken in general terms, except a few digressions, which I thought necessary to fully understand the subject.

This is now the fourth expedition that Captain Marcy has accomplished, with honour and credit to himself, and to the satisfaction of the government. Major Neighbours had lived the best years of his life upon the frontier, and had spent fourteen years in intimate relation with the wild Indians. Dr. Shumard had the experience of the Red River trip under Captain Marcy, besides being well versed in geology, mineralogy, and natural history; whilst the corps of Indian hunters and guides were themselves efficient by birth and habit, and led by a Delaware of intelligence and great experience, whose traits and stories of Indian life were imparted with freedom, and every reason for full reliability.

With such advantages, I trust I have made a book, reliable for what information it may contain, and entertaining, from the incidents I have endeavoured to combine with what might be otherwise considered dry detail.

FORT SMITH TO THE CHOCTAW AGENCY.

---◆---

CHAPTER I.

Act of Texas Legislature.—Capt. Marcy ordered to take Command.—Departure from New York.—Arrival at Fort Smith.—Fitting out the Train.—Departure for Fort Washita.—Incidents of the first two days.

THE great drawback to rapid settlement beyond the frontier of the South and West, is the depredations committed by the roving bands of Indians, who subsist in that region. These people live an entirely nomadic life, have no settled homes, wander from place to place over the vast plains in search of game or plunder, and living in this precarious way, are necessarily often reduced to a state of starvation. As they live entirely upon flesh, large quantities are of course consumed, and when reduced to short allowance, they eat horses and mules. This, together with the necessity of having animals to transport themselves and families, also to use in war and the chase, induces constant forays upon exposed situations, when murder, rapine and captivity are the inevitable results to the hapless settler. Many well cultivated spots have thus been broken up and abandoned, and the continuance of the evil retards emigration and enterprize to such an extent that large tracts of the most fertile kind are left tenantless.

To remove this scourge from *her* territory, the State of

Texas, by an act of her Legislature, approved Feb. 6th, 1854, appropriated eighteen square leagues of her unlocated lands, to form a reserve, for the settlement of all the Indians within her borders, on condition that the United States government would cause these lands to be located and surveyed, and would induce the Indians to settle upon them, confine themselves to their limits, go to farming, and quit their wandering and predatory habits,—the United States government also agreeing to send agricultural implements, seeds, men to teach the Indians to farm and take care of stock, and subsistence for the Indians until a crop was raised.

The Secretary of War, and Secretary of the Interior, issued orders in April of the same year, to Captain Marcy, then in New York, to repair forthwith to Fort Smith, on the frontier of Arkansas, and organize an expedition to carry out the provisions of this act.

The previous reputation of this officer, his long experience and thorough knowledge of prairie and frontier life, eminently qualified him for this duty, connected with which he was also required to penetrate the *terra incognita* at the head waters of the Big Washita and Brazos rivers, explore these streams to their sources, and ascertain the description of country where they take their rise.

The long and friendly intimacy that had existed between the Captain and myself, afforded me an opportunity to realize what has been to me the dream of my whole life, viz., a tour over the vast plains of the far South-west; and it was with no little pleasure and self-congratulation that I availed myself of it, as I should have, not only an intimate friend of noble spirit, energy and experience for my companion and director, but also the sanction and protection of the government. As may be supposed, no persuasion was necessary, and though the time was short, my preparations were soon made.

Captain Marcy's orders arrived on the 26th of April, and on the 4th of May we left New York, arriving in Fort Smith on the 18th, when the Captain, with his accustomed energy, aided by the efficient Quartermaster, Captain French, immediately set about his preparations, and with such perseverance and success, that by the 1st of June we were ready for our long journey.

The town of Fort Smith, (in the suburbs of which stands the garrison,) is a place of considerable commercial importance, doing a large Indian and up river trade. It stands upon the Arkansas river, near the mouth of the Poteau, and contains about twenty-five hundred inhabitants.

The garrison is well and substantially built of brick, and was at the time, the head quarters of the seventh infantry, commanded by Colonel Wilson, who, during the Mexican war was governor of Vera Cruz. This officer, took a deep interest in the expedition, (as he does in everything national,) and to him, we were indebted for many civilities, during our short stay.

The Captain here secured the services of Dr. G. G

Shumard (a resident physician of Fort Smith,) who accompanied him on his Red river exploration, as surgeon and naturalist, and joined us in the same capacity. He was an ardent enthusiast in the cause of science and, most indefatigable in its pursuit.

By orders, we were to get our military escort at Fort Arbuckle, about one hundred and twenty miles west, but the Captain determined, to march with our train through the Choctaw county to Fort Washita and meet the escort there, as the road was smoother, and more travelled—a great difference in our favor, with our heavy train.

June 1st.—We left Fort Smith at noon, and crossing the Poteau river, immediately in rear of the garrison, entered upon the Choctaw Reserve, " en route" for Fort Washita, one hundred and eighty miles distant.

Our train consisted of nine wagons, containing provisions, ammunition, camp equipage, small stores, and every thing necessary for our journey. Each of these was drawn by three yokes of oxen; we had, besides, ten horses, an ambuance drawn by two mules, and fifteen men, as teamsters, lartificers, cooks and hostlers.

The road, which was narrow, with but a single track, ran through a rich alluvial bottom, overgrown with a dense, luxuriant growth of wild cane and immense cotton-wood trees, and owing to the prevalence of late rains, was one quagmire for ten miles.

Our oxen, (unaccustomed to their drivers, and to a service

which, from the depth of the road, was so entirely different
from steady farm work,) proved very refractory, so it was
not long before two wagons were broken down, and to add
to our difficulties, a violent storm arose, of wind, rain, hail,
thunder, and lightning, fully realizing the truth of the old
adage, "it never rains but it pours."

Owing to these circumstances, and finding no convenient
place to encamp, (the whole country being flooded,) it was not
until ten P. M., that we reached a short prairie, twelve miles
upon our route, where wet and hungry, with the rain pouring
down in torrents, we found that the disabled wagons (which
we were obliged to leave in the swamp until they could be
repaired,) contained our camp baggage and rations, so that
we were obliged to resign ourselves to a supperless bed, upon
the wet grass, until the morning, thus making my initiation
into camp life, rather laborious and exciting, but far from
pleasant.

An incident during our march, amused and cheered me
very much.

Whilst riding along by the train, my ears were startled
by an old familiar air, and I found the amateur was one of
our ox drivers. He was carolling a moonlight love ditty,
whilst wading mid leg in mud. *Sentiment under difficulties;*
I knew not which to admire most, the song, or the happy
spirits of the singer; he seemed to admire, and feel quite
satisfied with both, judging from the hearty will with which
he appealed to moonlight, music, love and flowers. Surely, a

2*

poetical ox driver is an anomaly for a more unpoetical occupation cannot be imagined.

June 2d.—Towards morning, the storm subsided, but when day dawned, four horses and one yoke of oxen were missing. I mounted my horse to search for them, having previously despatched a party to assist in getting up the wagons from the swamp. In the course of my ride, I met with a very agreeable surprise at an Indian house by the roadside, where I stopped to make some inquiries.

My attention had been arrested in passing this house, during the storm and darkness of the previous night, by a merry ringing laugh, and cheerful conversation. On stopping this morning, I was met by a kind and courteous welcome from one of the inmates, (whose voice I recognized as the same,) who hearing my story, invited me to breakfast, and made me quite forget my cares, in the charm of her society. A prairie flower, brought up and educated upon the frontier, she had never been in a town of any size in her life, but though ignorant of the world, and forms of society, I found her a proud specimen of native grace, intelligence, and affability. A Cherokee, she owed her improvement in mind, to the excellent institution founded by Ross, at Talaqua, her manners, however, were the result of no convention, but the gift of birth and blood. The daughter of a distinguished chief of her tribe, her soul was full of the ancient nobility of her race, whilst filled with indignation at their wrongs and present degradation, and her eye kindled, and her tongue became eloquent whilst dwelling upon their ancient grandeur. I was charmed beyond measure, surprised to a degree, for with a majority, I had hitherto considered Indian worth and character, a matter of tradition ; it was like sunset upon a ruin, or like the last strains of distant melody, which linger upon the ear as if loathe to leave. Subsequent experience has proven to me, however, that she was but one in a thousand,— the death knell of Indian greatness has sounded, and ere long he will have vanished forever from the scene.

The wagons coming up I was obliged to leave, when she proposed to accompany me a short distance, as she wished to visit a sick person in the neighborhood. Taking down an excellent double barrelled gun, and equipping herself regularly for hunting, with powder and shot flasks, gamebag, &c., she smiled at my surprised look, and remarked, " I hope to have the opportunity to show you I can use them," and so she did, as a squirrel and two quails were the result of her unerring aim and steady nerves, in the short space,—half a mile,—that she accompanied me.   With this double battery of eyes and arms, wo betide a susceptible bachelor, so thought I, but in my case it was *Ulysses and Calypso*, so bidding adieu to my quondam syren, I galloped off to the unromantic drudgery of the camp.   Arriving there, I found the missing oxen and horses had been brought in, and all hands busy in preparing a hearty meal, after which tents were pitched, and we spent a comfortable night.

The prairie, on which we were encamped, was about

three miles wide, destitute of trees, but covered with rich grass, and beautiful flowers, among which the prairie pink, shone conspicuous, also a species of blue flag, very delicate, I made some selections of both. The soil was a dark loam.

CHAPTER II.

CHOCTAW AGENCY TO GAINES' CREEK.

Arrive at the Agency.—Law against introduction of whiskey among the Indians.—
Ball play.—Profanity among teamsters.—Description of an Indian family and
hut.—Accident to wagon.—Meeting of friends.—Pass the narrows.—Bituminous
coal found.—Emigrants grave.—Night in an Indian hut.—The sub-Chief and
his peculiarities.—Arrival at the Fouche Maliant.—Arrival at the Council-
House.—Singular pottery found.—Description of prairie scenery.—Flies troublesome —Mutiny among teamsters.—Detention of train.—Description of the
Indian in his home.

June 3rd.—A start at noon to day, brought us to the Choctaw Agency at five P. M., where we witnessed—accidentally
—a painful, though necessary execution of the laws of the
United States, against the introduction of whiskey among the
Indians. The penalty is severe, viz., fine, imprisonment,
confiscation of the whiskey, and in case of negroes, flogging,
at the discretion of the authorities. We had previously seen
two negroes chained together by the neck, and driven along
the road, by several men ; these proved to be the offenders,
the one a freeman, the other a slave. It is optional with the
owner, to allow the slave to be whipped or not, (the alternative
being expulsion from the nation,) and in this instance he
declined, but the free negro was undergoing the infliction of
sixty lashes, laid on with an unmerciful hand, and to judge by
his groans and cries, the punishment was full expiation for the
offence.

This law has had a very good effect, and enlisting as it does the pride and energies of the Indians themselves, it creates a spirit of emulation among them, in this way, viz., a police force is organized, called the Light Horse, under pay from the general government. Their duty is a general one, but particularly to seize and destroy all liquor introduced upon the reserve either for sale or private use. To be Captain of the Light Horse is a post of great honor, and is a source of much rivalry among the young men of the nation, thus thoroughly identifying them with this praiseworthy effort to remove a scourge from the red man, more terrible in its consequences to him than death. The same law is enforced, in regard to all Indians within the boundaries of the States and Territories, and though often evaded has had an infinite salutary effect in reducing crime and distress among them.

The little town of Scullyville, where the agency is located, is a collection of log tenements, principally stores, where a large Indian trade is done. It stands about a mile from an extensive prairie, the road to which, like that from our late encampment, ran over a succession of hills of sand and clay covered with low post oaks.

Upon entering upon the prairie, we observed in the distance a crowd of natives in gay clothing, the brilliant colours blending with the verdure, and making at sunset a truly picturesque scene. Riding up, we witnessed a scene never to be forgotten. It was a ball-play. Described, as this sport has been, by the able pencil of Catlin, description falls far short of reality. About six hundred men, women and children, were assembled, all dressed in holiday costume, and all as intent upon the game as it is possible to be where both pleasure and interest combine. The interest, is one tribe against another, or one county of the same tribe, against a neighboring county ; the pleasure, that which savages always take in every manly and athletic sport. In this instance the contestants were all Choctaws, practising for their annual game with the Creeks, and I was struck with the interest taken by all the lookers on, in the proficiency of each of the players. About sixty on each side were engaged in this exciting play, than which no exercise can be more violent nor better calculated to develope muscle and harden the frame. Each player provides himself with what are called ball-sticks. They are in shape like a large spoon, made of a piece of hickory about three feet long, shaved thin for about nine inches at the end forming the spoon, then bent round until brought into shape, the end securely fastened to the handle by buckskin thongs, the under side or bottom of the spoon covered with a coarse net work of the same material. He has one in each hand, and the ball—about the size of a large marble, is held between the spoons and thrown with an overhand rotary motion, separating the spoons, when the top of the circle is reached.

The game is this—Two poles are set up, each about seventeen feet high and a foot apart at the bottom, widening to three feet at top. At the distance of two hundred yards, two similar poles are set up facing these. To strike the poles, or throw the ball between them counts one, and twelve is game. An umpire and starter takes the ball, advances to a mark equi-distant from each end of the course, and throws it vertically into the air; it is caught, or falling upon the ground is eagerly struggled for and thrown toward the desired point. We saw some throw the ball the whole distance.

At each brace of poles, judges are stationed, who, armed with pistols, keep close watch, and whenever a count is made fire their pistols. The ball is then taken and started anew.

Among the players, are the runners, the throwers, and those who throw themselves in the way and baffle the player who succeeds in getting the ball.

The runners are the light active men, the throwers heavier, and then the fat men, who can neither throw nor run, stand ready to seize a thrower or upset a runner.

When a runner gets the ball, he starts at full speed towards the poles; if intercepted, he throws the ball to a friend, a thrower, perhaps, he is knocked down, then begins the struggle for the ball; a scene of pushing, jostling, and striking with the ball sticks, or perhaps a wrestle or two, all attended with hard knocks and harder falls. Whilst looking on, one man was pitched upon his head and had his collar bone broken; another, had part of his scalp knocked off, but it was all taken in good humour, and what, among white men, would inevitably lead to black eyes and bloody noses, here ended with the passage or possession of the ball, a good lesson in forbearance and amiability, worthy of imitation.

The combatants are stripped entirely naked except a breech cloth and moccasins, and gaudily painted; they fasten at the centre and small of the back, a horse's tail, gaily painted and arrayed like a tail that has been knicked by a jockey ; some wore bouquets of flowers instead of the tail, but these were evidently the exquisites of the party, which the rings worn in the ears, nose and under lips, and manner of arranging the hair—one having it cut to a point and drawn down over his right eye, whilst his left eye was painted green—clearly proved. The grotesque appearance of the players, the excitement, yells and shouts of the crowd, old and young, and the gaudy finery displayed, all combined to make an indelible impression upon our memories. The aged men of the tribe were the most noisy and excited. One old fellow, blind of an eye and seventy years old, was quite wild with excitement ; shaking his red handkerchief, he continued to shout, hoo, ka, li—hoo, ka, li— catch, catch, when the ball was thrown, and chi, ca, ma,— good, when a count was made, until quite hoarse. Doubtless, like the old war horse at the sound of the bugle, he felt all the fire of his youth, as he entered into the full spirit of this truly and only Indian sport.

With reluctance we were obliged to leave for our quiet camp in the same prairie, and until nightfall, could hear the yells and laughter of the retiring crowd.

June 4th. This (the first extensive prairie we had met) was about seven miles wide, surrounded by timber, and covered with flowers, among which the marigold and clematis were profuse; the soil was quite sandy. At dawn of day we were again "en route." It was a beautiful sight in the dim light and bracing air of morning, to see the long line of white covered wagons rolling quietly over the slopes of the prairie; the lowing of the oxen, the snorting of the horses, the shouts and cracking of whips by the drivers, with all the bustle of breaking up camp made up an enlivening scene, which must be experienced to be enjoyed. One thing however marred its enjoyment to me, and that was the awful profanity of the drivers. I have often since had occasion to comment upon and reprove this among this class of men, but never has it struck me as so ill-timed and unnatural as when indulged in, in the midst of natural beauties, which might fire a dying hermit; under such circumstances—blasphemy (a practice senseless, sinful and unnecessary) is like a volcano, devastating the fair fields, and sunny vineyards, of Italian climes, harrowing to the soul, revolting to nature.

Being quite unwell—the result of the severe exposure of the last few days, I stopped in the course of the morning at an Indian hut to get some coffee, and had an opportunity to make some observations upon the indolence, carelessness, want of calculation and slovenly habits of this semibarbarous people. The man had built his hut, which was new, about half as large as was necessary to accommodate his family, consisting of five adults and four children, and even this he was too indolent to finish. It had but one room, built of logs, roofed with a rude clap board, split from sapling oak. The floor was laid in puncheons—logs hewn on one side. He had hewed enough to cover all but a four feet square hole in the centre, this was left open, and being convenient, was used as a receptacle for offal and a lounging place for dogs, of which I subsequently ascertained there are always a host about every Indian house. One can judge of the atmosphere of such a place.—Here they ate, drank and slept, and as philosophers say that man's comfort consists in his idea of what constitutes comfort, managed to live.

One of the squaws made coffee in an iron skillet, stirring it with an oaken paddle; when poured out it was of the consistency of corn gruel, but having called for it, I gulped it down for fear of giving offence, and paying my dime took my departure ; my opinion, however, formed at the time, I have had no occasion to change from subsequent observations among them.

Our road, after leaving the prairie, ran over a succession of rough stony hills, covered with low oak trees. In descending one, the foremost wagon was disabled by the breaking· of an axle-tree, and as the road was too narrow to pass, we were obliged to look out for camping ground, where there was water and grass to last until the damage could be repaired. These we found a quarter of a mile in advance, in a swamp, on the banks of the Brazil ; so unhitching our oxen and unsaddling horses, we prepared to encamp. Shortly after a severe rain storm set in, so that with wet, gnats and mosquitoes, &c., the evening promised to be anything but pleasant, when just as we began to feel very melancholy, I thought I heard a familiar voice, and going to the door of the tent, who should I meet but my old friend S. H———s, whom I had not seen for sixteen years. He was on his way to Fort Washita, and having been thrown from his horse in the prairie—the horse escaping—had made his way on foot to our camp—stange coincidences happen in life, but this was a joyful one for he and I, that after so many years and changes in fortune, we should meet by accident in this wild Indian country, to fight over our battles by the camp fire's light. Had he dropped from the clouds, I could not have been more surprised, certainly not more delighted, and in spite of rain and insects, we spent a lively evening. We supplied him with a horse, and he remained with us several days.

June 5th.—Repairs to the broken wagon detained us until a late hour this morning. We got off at ten, A. M., and crossing the swollen Brazil, passed through several short prairies variegated with the wild sun-flower, marygold and wild-rose. A few hours brought us to the Narrows, where the road ran through a rugged mountain gorge, very difficult for wagons. The locality is interesting from its geological formation. We found a vein of bituminous coal seventeen inches thick, and numerous fossils of limestone, the soil being argillaceous. Near the road, we passed an emigrant's grave, covered with a pent house of logs, and marked by the tail-board of a wagon, nailed upon a stake, upon which was rudely written with tar, " George Bemshaus, born in Prussia, October

13th, 1812 ; died, March 2d, 1854." Poor fellow! all his hopes of home and fortune in the land of freedom, lay here on a barren hill-side in this wild Indian country,—such is life, a vision, a struggle, a grave.

Before leaving Fort Smith, the Captain had taken the precaution to procure some corn, to feed our oxen until they became accustomed to such hard work, instead of depending entirely upon grass diet. This supply was now exhausted, and H———s and myself started in advance to procure more. Stopping at a noted place—Tushcounti's—we were told we could purchase some three miles farther on—we found—and I have since constantly observed—that these people have no idea of distance. When one gets information of this kind from them, it is best to multiply by two and add the original quantity, even then sometimes—as in our case—falling short of the fact. We rode twelve miles and then stopped for the night at an Indian hut. As we had eaten nothing since morning, we asked if we could have eggs and chickens for supper, having seen plenty of the feathered bipeds about, and were answered in the affirmative. With appetites sharpened by our exercise and long fast, we came to supper and found the eggs served up on the only piece of family plate, 'tis true, a glass dish, but fried in *tallow*, the chickens fried in the same, and a dish of sausages, made of the intestines of the hog, dried in the sun, a meal which a man might eat when in imminent danger of starvation, but which our day's fast had not quite toned our appetites to. We took a cup of coffee—the only

3*

thing *swallowable*, and went to the door to smoke and look at the moon, the odour of the viands being quite sufficient. Next, came our accommodations for the night. The hut had no windows in it, but to avoid stumbling over the living, snoring crew upon the floor, a pine knot blazed upon the hearth, and here, stowed in one corner, lay the Indian, his squaw, his daughter about nineteen years old, two young papooses, a negro slave with an infant at the breast, and two dogs, whilst on a kind of shelf, raised about two feet from the floor, were perched the writer and his friend, with our saddles for pillows, and our horse blankets for covering, for this privilege we paid two dollars.*

June 6th.—When morning dawned, we wished to make our usual ablutions, but found that basin and towels, were not known in the domestic list; however the squaw offered us an old bake pan and a piece of cotton cloth, which she pulled off of a bundle in the hut, we declined the *novelty*, and preferred

---

*In this country, and all through the South and West, prices are much higher than in the East, and from what seems to me, to be an unfair cause, viz., the smallest general currency, is the dime, but where five and three cent pieces are used, they are taken each to be of the value of the other; now I noticed in a town in Arkansas, where a shrewd fellow took advantage of this, in this way:—In making change he would be sure to give three cent pieces where fives were due, and take fives where he was entitled to but threes; then, when visiting New Orleans, to make purchase of goods, he would buy up three cent pieces to use in the same way. To be sure, it was but a small business, but turned out a large per centage in proportion.

Cents are never seen, and thus, though you get nothing better for your money, you pay just this proportionate advance for it. Whether this arises from the greater abundance of money, or the enlarged views of the population, I leave for those to judge who are better able than myself.

contenting ourselves until we joined the train. It was necessary to have some breakfast, however; so taking the experience of the supper for our guide, we superintended the boiling of some eggs in the shells, and with some corn dodgers and coffee made out very well.

Much to our surprise and satisfaction, our quondam host, who enjoyed the high-sounding name of George Washington, stirred himself this morning and procured from a neighbor what corn we wanted, so we waited here until the train came up. This neighbor called over to see us, and afforded us much amusement. He was a sub-chief of his tribe, and was indulging in one of his periodical debauches. " I am a first rate fellow but I must have whiskey," said he; " how often do you get drunk?" said I. He replied, " once every three months." " How long does it last ?" *Ans.* " About two months." " Well then, you are drunk more than half the time ?" *Ans.* " Oh yes, nearly all the time, but then *the old woman*, she keeps things in order." So it is with the victim of self-indulgence, in savage, as well as civilized life, *the old woman*, is left to keep things in order.

Happening to mention the ball-play, he fired up at once, as it turned out he was quite a sporting man, and was in the habit of betting heavily upon the result of these contests, (at which, by the way, large sums of money, also horses and mules, change hands,) and of course was well booked up. " Them Scullyville fellows can't come it over our county," said he, ' We can just take and lam them out of their boots." Ha, ha, the Bowery among the Indians, we both laughed heartily at the idea, and were not a little surprised to find he had never been off the Reserve in his life, so that slang seems to be a native gift. After a few more swigs at his friend's jug, the sub-chief retired to the bushes, if not great like kings, " still quite as glorious, o'er all the ills of life victorious," and, judging by his sonorous snoring, would soon be prepared for a new attack upon the enemy.

Soon after the sub-chief's departure, the train came up, when we joined and crossed the Fouche Maliant, a stream which empties into Red River, remembered as the vicinity where a horrid murder was committed during the march of the escort to the expedition to New Mexico, in 1849. This murder, illustrating, as it does, the demoniac spirit of the Indian when actuated by revenge, is worthy of note. The circumstances are these, and show clearly that *Lex Talionis* is *de facto* the only law recognized by the Indian.

One of the soldiers, attached to the escort, killed a hog belonging to a family in the neighborhood, at which they were greatly enraged. When the officer in command, the lamented H——n, was informed of the matter, he returned and paid an exorbitant price for the animal. This seemed satisfactory, but on the following morning, two of the party were found murdered with tomahawks. The supposition is, that emissaries were sent out (in revenge,) and sufficient time did not allow of their recal after the hog was paid for.

The young officer mentioned, afterwards met with a tragical end, from his misplaced confidence in the Indians in New Mexico.

A man of extraordinary amiability and goodness of heart, he had often expressed his conviction that the Indian only wanted a display of confidence reposed in him by the white man to cause him to fraternize. Fatal mistake ! and one that cost him his life. Some months after the event recorded above, he left camp, and not returning at the time expected, search was made for him, when his dead body was found, scalped and stripped.

Everything indicated that he had endeavoured to carry out his favourite theory, the commanding officer of the expedition having made a thorough examination of the ground where the murder was committed, with the aid of his Indian guide, (the results of which are given in the note appended,*) and followed the murderers forty miles, when, owing to the disabled condition of his horses and mules, he was obliged to return.

* The sagacity of the Delaware guide is shown in the minute details of his report of this investigation. The result is as follows :

This murder was committed by two men. They had two mules and one horse with them. They came down upon their victim at full gallop, but finding that he was not disposed to fly, but on the contrary walked his horse towards them, they also pulled up to a walk. The parties met and rode a short distance together, then dismounted, and seating themselves on the grass, smoked together. Here they got possession of his rifle, on pretence, as supposed, of examining it. As this was the only weapon he had with him, they then over-powered, tied him, and placing him upon his horse, led the horse between them into some timber, skirting a ravine, where one falling behind, shot him in the back of his head, the ball found in the brain, indicating that the deed was com-

Subsequent experience has proved to me that the invariable rules for safety, that should be followed by single individuals or small parties, when away from camp, and meeting parties of Indians, is to give them a wide berth, and for this reason—if sheer plunder is not the object of attack, according to their custom, young men cannot hold any position in their tribe, until they can show a scalp, and have stolen a number of horses. In consequence of this, two or three will start together, and sometimes be absent for a year, until they can return with these evidences of their manliness.

The best plan is either to make the escape to camp, or else preserving a bold front, take care to have the first shot.

Had young H——n observed these directions, so often impressed upon him by his experienced commanding officer, he might now be living, an ornament to the service, to which he was a great loss, as he was mounted upon a horse remarkable for fleetness, and was a crack shot with the rifle.

A few miles travel brought us to the deserted Council House of the nation, at the time occupied by an Indian

mitted with his own rifle. Hastily stripping him, they scalped him, threw his body into a ravine, and taking everything but one boot and his saddle, made their escape. Some miles farther they halted, and lighting a fire, had prepared some meat for cooking, as the raw meat was found spitted and the fire smoul. dering. They left here very hastily, as a pair of moccasins, a lariat, and some other articles were dropped in their hurry, occasioned doubtless by hearing the report of the howitzer which was fired from camp at sun-down as a guide to the missing officer.

Minute as these details are, they are true, as the murderers are known, and will sooner or later be brought to justice. All the Indian had to direct him was the signs in the grass, &c.

family, the place of assembling in Council having been changed to Doaxville, farther south.

It was a long, rambling building, built of logs, and not different, except in size, from their ordinary houses. Here I dug up a singular piece of pottery, of an antique form, and covered with various devices, but was unable to get any information about it from the family. They said they had never seen anything like it before, and did not know how it came there. Its shape and whole appearance proved it to be very ancient.

Our road from the stream was gradually ascending, and bounded on both sides by timber, when of a sudden we reached the top of the ridge and had a view of the largest prairie we had yet met. O, the glorious beauty of that scene. Fancy would in vain attempt to paint it! Below, stretching for twenty-five miles in length, and twelve in breadth, lay a sea of pale green, hemmed in by timber of a darker hue; flowers of every variety, shade and form, interspersed over the surface; a dark green belt of verdure here and there, marking the ravines and water-courses, and groves of trees, or clumps, or single trees, scattered in such perfect arrangement over the whole, as to seem as though some eminent artist had perfected the work. And truly so he did, for what artist can compare with the God who formed and arranged all these natural beauties now spread before us!

The view, fully realized descriptions of the parks of the English nobility and gentry, wanting only the presence of animal life. Its effect upon us is best illustrated by the following incident.

Our whole command stopped involuntarily, in mute admiration; at last, one poor fellow, a rough, uncouth specimen of an ox driver burst, out, " Oh, if I was only *a lawyer*, how I could talk about such a sight as this, but I havn't the *larnin* to say what I want." Now, whether there is anything peculiar in the legal profession, which gives a higher zest to enjoyment of the beautiful in nature, I confess I do not know, of one thing I am certain, that lawyer or doctor, saint or sinner, any man who could gaze upon and not admire a scene like this, must be wanting in the very elements of the division between the human and animal.

As every pleasure has its pain, every joy its sorrow, our feelings of admiration for the scenery, were soon merged into those of pity, for our horses, mules and oxen.

The great drawback to pleasure, at this season, on the prairie, is the immense number of insects. Among these, is a large, greenish brown horse fly, the most inveterate blood sucker of the genus. So ravenous are they, that, after settling down to their bloody work, they will allow themselves to be picked up in the fingers, making no effort to escape. At every stroke of their bills, the blood flows as if from a lancet, and they come in such myriads, that I have seen a horse bathed in his own blood. An idea prevails, that they will attack a white horse, or mule, sooner than any other color, but this I think erroneous, and doubtless arises from the fact, that the marks of blood, are more visible upon the white hair, also white animals, are generally thinner skinned, and consequently more sensitive.

It has often been a matter of reflection to me, why this torment should have been inflicted upon dumb brutes. My conclusion is, that it is intended for man, as an exercise of his humanity.

As we passed only along the edge of the prairie, we were soon through safely, though we had a busy time fighting the tormentors, and entering a shady road, had proceeded but a short distance before we were stopped by the sudden announcement of five of our teamsters, that they would go no farther. These men, living a precarious but indolent life, upon the frontier of Arkansas, had joined the expedition with very romantic ideas, but the realities and discipline of camp life had cured them, and go any farther they would not; but leaving us upon the hill side, they turned their faces towards their accustomed lounging places, and were gone. We made out to work along a few miles, by all turning in as teamsters, and reaching a large farm, occupied by an old Indian, halted until we could hire more help—a change which we often afterwards congratulated ourselves upon.

The evening set in with a violent rain storm; so, to be as comfortable as possible during our detention, we took possession of an untenanted house on the premises, and building a fire in the hearth (for it was quite cold), we spread our blankets upon the floor and resigned ourselves to sleep, after a very good meal of milk, eggs, chickens, &c., which we procured from the farm house.

Though annoyed at this unexpected detention, by which we lost three days' travel, we were enabled during our stay to observe the Indian in his home, and to form our own opinions of his enterprize and moral worth,—an opportunity I had long wished for.

At an Indian house we passed to-day, I observed some little negroes, from two years old and under. They were naked, and were most singular and unsightly objects, from the distortion and protuberance of the stomach and abdomen. This is attributable to their being fed entirely on corn bread, causing enlargement of the spleen and other distresses. On speaking of this circumstance to the owner, he said, " Well, may be so dey live, may be not ;" a matter of indifference to him, whose own stomach seemed well fed and healthy enough, but upon whom the natural consequences of cause and effect made no impression.

June 7th, 8th and 9th.—Our quondam host was a full-blooded Choctaw. He served in the Creek war with General Jackson, and like all of his tribe, was very proud of the fact that they have always been allies of the United States. His wealth in cattle and horses, besides money (which was all hoarded, never, as is a general thing with Indians, put out at interest), was said to be over one hundred thousand dollars, and yet he was living not only in a filthy but most uncomfortable and disgusting manner, fond of nothing but gold and silver, which when we paid him the few dollars of expense incurred, he clutched with all the gloating of a miser, and shook with tremulous delight as he told them one by one into his greasy bag. We wanted some corn for our animals during our stay, and when asked for it, he denied having any to spare at first. This proved to be a "*ruse*" to raise the price, for as the market price was one dollar per bushel, so soon as we expressed our willingness to give one dollar and a half, he shrugged his shoulders, and very quietly said, " Well, as blackberry come soon—may be so—you can have him," at the same time pointing the way to two well filled cribs.

The use of these berries is an evidence of the improvidence of the Indian, as I am told a large number depend upon them in a great measure ; in fact, I heard one sturdy chap say, " Well, I got corn till blackberry come, then may be so corn be d——d ;" and in conversation with our host, he said that the corn in the neighborhood was almost entirely consumed, and the present season promised badly, but ' may be so dey git some blackberry, may be not." This was said with an indifferent shrug, as if the prospect or the reality of starvation around him was a matter of no consequence.

Many visitors came to the farm during our stay. All, of course, visited our quarters, and sat or stood around in that quiet manner peculiar to the Indian, and which, I think, conceals a great deal of curiosity, of which they are supposed to be guiltless. One, a fine looking youth, gaily dressed and painted, with his hair cut "a la roundhead," had a good deal to say, in his broken way. I asked him his name; he said " George." " Well, George what?" I asked. " Why, *George*, may be so George be good name 'nough;" and this was all the satisfaction I got for my inquiry.

Some of the visitors got up a dance one evening. There were six dancers—three squaws and three men. The music was a droning discordance of sounds, drawn from an old cracked fiddle by the husband of one of the squaws, and the dance consisted in a monotonous bobbing up and down, like a bear on a hot plate, accompanied by yells, which grew louder as the night waxed older, and the whiskey began to take effect, so that long after we had retired to our blankets, we were roused when a louder yell than usual pealed out, or a heavier stamping announced that the orgie was becoming more fast and furious.

We met with, and in use, at this place, some vessels of the same material and ancient shape, as the one I had previously dug up at the deserted Council House. Our host told us they were made of an admixture of clay and pounded muscle shells, but the art of making them was lost. They will stand the fire and would answer for crucibles as well as cooking pots.

It rained heavily at intervals during our stay, and one evening, during a heavy shower, I went to the door of our quarters and observed a large fire burning near some out-buildings. On inquiry, I learned it was the old man's *bivouac*. Being curious to investigate the matter further, we went over, despite the rain, and found this old creature, seventy years old, and suffering with the liver complaint, stretched near the fire, upon a bundle of skins and old blankets, with no shelter but the overhanging eaves. It had been his habit from infancy to sleep in the open air, and he said he could not sleep in a house. The doctor offered him medical aid for his complaint, but he declined, being either too stingy or too superstitious to avail himself of it. He said, "No, no—our man he do dat—he good 'nough;" meaning their medicine man, to whom they still adhere.

One morning we heard a great commotion in the stock yard, and going over, found that some young colts were to be branded. We witnessed the process done in true Indian style, the animal being first lassoed and choked until powerless, then thrown, the branding iron applied, and an inch of the tail cut off, to make it lighter and more under control of the colt to brush off insects. It is then liberated, frightened half to death, and, I have no doubt, injured by the brutal manner in which it has been handled.

They pursued this process of branding with all their stock except their hogs. The hogs roamed in the woods, and lived on Mast,* or starved to death if that failed ; no care was taken to improve the breed, and those met with, were a long-nosed, long-legged, slab-sided species, black in color, and evidently descendants of the wild hog, or peccary. This old man had about one thousand head in his range, and seemed

* Mast is the nut of the oak and beach trees.

4*

to think he would be able to save enough to last him in his family, as hog and hominy was their only diet.

Of cattle and horses, the old man had a large herd, in fact, he told me he did not know the number, but "sometime de boy he count 'em." The calves were all kept in an enclosure, and thus the cows were induced to return from pasture, when enough milk was taken for butter, &c., the rest allowed to the calves. I could not help but think what a handsome account one of our New England farmers would turn such a dairy to.

An incident occurred during the branding, which affected me very much, and which I will now relate :

When all the large colts had been branded, a beautiful milk-white filly, four years old, with a colt six weeks old, at her foot, was driven up. At first she made every effort to escape, guarding the colt at the same time, but soon the colt was lassoed and thrown, instantly, she stopped, and standing the very picture of agony, with glaring eyeballs and distended nostrils, trembling in every limb and muscle of her frame, and the sweat running off her in a stream, uttering all the time a low, whining moan, presented a picture of distress, which, in a dumb brute, was as affecting as it was extraordinary. As soon as the colt was liberated, she sprang forward, and caressing it with all the affection of a mother, bounded off into the woods, taking care to keep it in front and in sight of her; truly, thought I, if any thing could create a belief in Metempsychosis, it would be sights like this.

Most of the Choctaws hold slaves, but my observations,

both here and elsewhere, have convinced me that the general government would subserve the cause of humanity by prohibiting any Indians from holding them; they look upon them as mere beasts of burden, and treat them accordingly.

At this place there were two slaves; one an old woman of seventy years of age, and lame with inflammatory rheumatism, the other a child of eight years old, who were compelled to do all the hard work about the farm. We saw the old woman sent out to catch and saddle a horse, and the boy, with no clothing on but a coarse, ragged, filthy tow shirt, chopping logs of wood, and then shouldering and carrying into the house, a log larger than himself.

Our sympathies were very much excited, and on remonstrating with the old man, and telling him that the boy would be strained and injured for sale, he merely shrugged his shoulders, and replied, "He strong 'nough, me work hard when me boy, me seventy year old, me strong yet."

One of the party gave the little fellow an old shirt, which he donned immediately, half wild with delight, and strutted off to show his prize, but he soon came back in tears, with the shirt hanging in ribbons about him, his unusual appearance having excited the anger of the big bull of the herd, and in making his escape, he lost the most of his finery in the bushes.

Another of our party offered to buy the boy, but the avaricious old wretch, immediately put up his price beyond his means, and upon being told that his price was unreasonable, merely replied, " He good boy, may be so, somebody give it for him, may be not."

Instances might be multiplied of great barbarities practised ; one, is that of an Indian in this nation, standing and enjoying the pastime of his half-grown boy, which consisted in practising with bow and arrows, at a negro boy, as a target. Another, ordered a slave to shoot a man against whom he had a grievance, and upon refusal, whipped the slave to death. These are not isolated cases, but good specimens of their estimation of, and general treatment of slaves, and would seem to prove conclusively, that the Indian needs a master, as much, if not more, than the slave.

June 10th.—Having succeeded in filling the places of our shameless deserters, we left the old man and his ill-enjoyed wealth, at an early hour this morning, and commenced the ascent of a steep, stony hill, on the opposite side of which slopes a prairie, extending down to Gaines' creek.

Just before we left, an incident occurred, showing the inherent laziness of the Indian. A stout, able-bodied man, equipped for hunting, and riding a beautiful white pony, came by, and stopped, in that peculiar quiet manner I have before remarked upon.

One of our party, pleased with the pony, asked the price. He raised his hands three times, with all the fingers extended, as much as to say, thirty dollars ; immediately the money was counted down, but he then declined selling his pony, saying, it was too far for him to walk home. " How far ?" was the question. " Five mile," was his reply. Forty dollars were then offered, but still, though it staggered him a good deal, he persisted in declining, as rather than walk five miles, he would forego the opportunity of selling his pony at so greatly an increased rate.

On reaching the creek, we found it too high to ford, and so encamped in a beautiful grove on the slope of the prairie, and a beautiful quiet evening we had, when the first clear moon for some nights, rose to hallow the peaceful scene below, the white tents, and the white covers of the wagons, peeping out from among the trees, the camp fires blazing, and the cattle feeding upon the green sward around us. We felt the soothing influence of the scene, after the rough times of the past week, and retired to our grassy couches with calmer thoughts for the morrow.

CHAPTER III.

JUNE 11th.—We found this morning, that the best horse
we had—a noble sorrel—had been struck by a snake in the
night, and could go no farther. The muscles of his throat
and fore-quarters, were so swollen that he could not raise his
head from the ground, so, reluctantly, we left him in charge
of a Choctaw, living in the vicinity, with directions to bring
him in to Fort Washita when he recovered. The doctor bled
him very freely in the mouth, and we made a muslin cover to
screen him from the flies, and so left him to his fate.

Instances of this kind are very frequent in this section of
country. The reptile is a small mottled snake, called Ground
Rattlesnake. This is a misnomer, as it has no rattles, and
strikes without warning. It is a species of the Copperhead,
its bite very venomous, and generally attended with fatal
results.

At ten A. M., (the water having subsided to a fordable
depth,) we crossed Gaines' Creek, and passing through several

beautiful prairies, rich in pasture, and covered with those beautiful flowers which always delighted us so much, (and through which we always roamed, making our selections,) and which we always parted from with regret, we came to a much more cultivated region. What first attracted our attention was a field of oats, a grain we had hitherto not met with, as the Indians raise nothing but corn. " Aha," said I, the "white man has had a hand in this," and so it proved to be the case. Several settlers from the States, who have married squaws, live here, the fact evidenced by the greater quantity of land cultivated, greater variety in the crops, the growth of vegetables, greater neatness about their buildings, and a general appearance of industry and thrift.

According to Choctaw law, no white man can marry until he has resided two years in the nation. He can then marry one of the tribe, and can fence in and cultivate as much as he pleases. There are many instances in the nation, and wherever met with, the difference from the native is very perceptible and striking.

Having learned, by the experience of the past, the phlebotomizing powers of the prairie-fly, we stopped at the first convenient place, and spent the rest of the day in making up muslin covers for our horses and mules, and during the day made some very interesting explorations and discoveries among the fossiliferous strata in the vicinity.

The soil is limestone, marked by the pellucid water and luxuriant vegetation. It yields, in ordinary seasons, forty bushels of grain to the acre; this season being unprecedently wet, the prospects were not so good.

Coal is found here in abundance, very bituminous, but used only by the few blacksmiths who live along the road.

A curious spectacle presented itself this morning, on our road. The whole surface of the ground, for more than a mile, was covered with the *army worm*, passing from one scene of devastation to another. They are about three inches long, white in colour, and lozenge shaped, travel slowly, but are a great scourge to the farmer, destroying—when they come in such hosts—in a night the labours of the season. Nothing but fire, I understand, has been able to check their ravages, and it is said that by burning off a narrow strip around a crop, it can be saved, as they will not cross burnt ground. My own impressions are, that as the larvæ are deposited by the insect after passing the chrysalis state, no means will be effectual, except they can be destroyed in the egg. This farmers North and East do, in case of the cutworm, by ploughing their land and subjecting it to the action of the weather.

June 12th.—At daylight we were on the road, and commenced passing through a more broken, but still well cultivated and flourishing country, as there is quite a settlement— if distances of from ten to fifteen miles can be called a settlement—of white men with squaw wives. An old Indian of some note also lived on this road. He was rich in cattle and horses, but, like his fellows, cultivated the soil to a very limited extent. We stopped for the night near a place where, on the twenty-eighth of May, a remarkable storm raged, destroying the crops and beating down timber.

Passing unobstructedly over so wide an extent, storms acquire terrific violence in this country, and leave indelible marks of their ravages.

One of the settlers, an intelligent white man, had sixty acres of oats destroyed, and told us that hail was thick enough, in some places, to be shovelled up. He said he measured some of the stones, and one was eight inches long and five in circumference, a fact which I believe, as I saw limbs of trees and their trunks skinned and battered as if by a discharge of grape shot. We procured here a fine hound to assist us in our catering when we got on the plains.

June 13th.—Our march to-day led us through an extensive prairie—covered as usual with a beautiful variety of flowers—where we found encamped a large party of emigrants, waiting for the subsidence of the waters of the Boggy, a stream more aptly named than pleasant to the traveller. They told us we could not cross, but we determined to make the attempt.

This stream ran through a bottom, which, in time of high freshet, was entirely submerged, leaving, as the water receded, a road which, though called bottom, seemed to have that necessary ingredient in a passable road entirely fallen out, or at least to require the race of men and animals found by that veracious traveller, Lemuel Gulliver, in the interesting country of Brobdignag, to find firm footing for travel.

A black, mucky deposit spread in width for two miles, and

5

our hapless party went floundering and plunging on, sometimes brought to a dead stand, anon sinking to the saddle
girths, then plunging into a slough and wondering what was
to come next, until bedaubed and bespattered, breathless and
half suffocated, we emerged upon the banks of the stream, and
cast an involuntary glance backwards to see whether we had
not left part of ourselves or our horses behind us.

With the loss of several horse and mule shoes, and the
breaking of a swingle tree in the ambulance, we got through,
and arriving on the banks of the stream found it too high to
cross with our wagons, and so set about to repair damages.

In course of the afternoon, we attempted to cross our horses
over by swimming them, but on account of the bad landing on
the opposite shore, were obliged to desist.

Having crossed myself, in a dug-out,* in anticipation of my
horse, I came near having an unpleasant adventure, viz., a
night alone in a Choctaw swamp.

Finding no likelihood of getting my horse, I started on foot
for Boggy Depot—a collection of dwellings and stores about
a mile from the stream—as the most comfortable place to
spend the night.

Indian-like, my guide gave me a direction, which, so far
from being direct, only made confusion worse confounded.

---

* A "dug-out" is a canoe made out of a solid log, the heart dug out with a
hatchet or adze, hence its name. The more primitive way of making them was
to burn them out, though there is no authority for saying that in consequence
these were called "burnt-outs."

The freshet had obliterated all marks of the road; but judging, I suppose, my instincts by his own, he pointed to a gap in the thicket, under a huge cottonwood, and grunting out, "You not miss him," left me to the tender mercies of gnats, mosquitoes, snakes, "et genus omne," which are only to be found in such a delectable place as Boggy Bottom.

I floundered on, every moment expecting to reach the welcome haven, but every step made it worse, until just as I was about to give up in despair, I heard the roar of a mill-dam, and hurrying on, found that I had boxed the compass and come round to the place I started from. I was glad to recross the stream and take up my quarters with the miller, where I found a blanket and a *soft punchin* to solace me after my unromantic ramble.

My host was quite wild upon the subject of a *diamond mine* he had found upon his premises; so after supper he produced his specimens, consisting of small quartz crystals imbedded in the harder rock, one of which he had extracted and fitted to a stick, to show how well it would cut glass; useless to him even for this, as glass for windows is unknown in this country. He looked blank when I told him the value of his prize, but to console him, I told him I would take some of the best specimens and have them well tested, giving him all the advantage that might result therefrom. I left him to his diamond dreams, and if there is pleasure in anticipation, I have no doubt this man thoroughly enjoys it.

June 14th.—The banks of the stream presented a wild and picturesque scene this morning.

A high, steep bluff, on the opposite shore, was lined with over a thousand head of wild cattle, about to be driven across, on their way to Missouri and Illinois.

These cattle are herded on the vast plains of Texas, until about three or four years old; they are then sold to men who follow the business, at from fifteen to eighteen dollars per head, driven to the prairies in the North-West, and there fattened for the Eastern market. They are very beautiful to look at, symmetrical in figure, with sinewy limbs, and very long, sharp-pointed horns.

Quite wild, the business of driving them is an arduous and a dangerous one. They go quietly enough until something occurs to excite or frighten them, when a stampede will occur, and woe betide the hapless wight who becomes involved in it; they become frantic, and bear down and crush every thing that stands in the way in their furious career.

The men who drive them, are a rough set, hardy and splendidly bold riders. I saw one catch his hat from the ground, when at full gallop, a feat which requires not only practice, but great muscle and dexterity. They ride a small horse, bred in Mexico, thick set and of great power of endurance.

The stock-whip they use, is a most formidable weapon; upon a short handle, about eighteen inches long, they fasten a plaited lash, from fifteen to eighteen feet in length, about an inch thick at the thickest part, tapering down to a very long thin end. Long practice enables them to throw this out, from its trail on the ground, with great accuracy and tremendous effect, cutting like a long flexible razor, and with a report like a pistol, drawing the blood at every blow.

It was an exciting sight, to see the herd plunge off the high bank—about fifteen feet perpendicular hight—and swim across, nothing appearing above water, but their taper heads and long thin horns. The emigrants we had passed upon the prairie had also come down, determined to cross at all hazards. They had exhausted all their provisions, and were too impatient to wait until the stream was fordable. There were about four hundred of them, men, women, and children, and the scene of confusion, and damage to property, beggars all description. Their goods were saturated with water, the whole party wetted to the skin; and in one instance a wagon sank entirely out of sight, and was only recovered by dint of diving and fastening ropes to it, when, with the assistance of several yokes of oxen, it was drawn ashore again.

Poor Richard says, " Two removes is as bad as a fire." I doubt whether the crossing of the Boggy was not a complete conflagration to these movers.

Emigration is very rapidly flowing into Texas, and of a class calculated materially to advance her interests. We conversed very freely with this party, and found them, both in outfit and conversation, a superior stock. They were all from Missouri, and had plenty of ready money.

5*

Their reason for emigrating was the cold and inhospitable climate of Missouri. One man told me that it was necessary to fodder cattle seven months in the year; a great difference to Texas, where cattle range in the pasture winter and summer, always fat and in good condition.

They all seemed to feel that the change they were making was a hazardous one, and indeed, when the difference in prices, the increased distance from market, and the risks run in acclimating, are taken into account, they might well think so; and I am satisfied, from what I saw and heard, that many a heartfelt regret was uttered for the home and comforts they had left.

My experience here and elsewhere, will always prompt me to give but one advice to persons disposed to emigrate, viz. : if you are comfortably off where you are, better stay, the contingencies are too great to warrant a change.

When Texas shall have completed a system of internal improvements, of course the objection of distance from market will not lie, and perhaps, as a stroke for posterity, these people were making a judicious move, but still, " let well enough alone," is a most excellent domestic motto.

Our heavy train, of course, could not pass the Boggy, and as it was the Captain's intention to stop, for a few days at all events, in the neighborhood of Fort Washita, until he could procure some more stock, let those we had rest, and await the arrival of our military escort from Fort Arbuckle ; we left our oxen and wagons on the prairie, and one of the party and myself, swam our horses and mules across, and started for Fort Washita (twenty-five miles distant), leading our spare horses, to procure for them good forage and attendance for a few days, previous to entering upon our long journey across the plains.

Did the reader ever undertake to lead a refractory horse, across an open country, in fly-time, with the thermometer at ninety-eight in the shade. If he did, he can fully sympathize with us, if he did not, he cannot feel a tithe of the excruciating torture of the operation.

The green flies—our quondam torturers—again made their appearance, and this time—it seemed to me—more famished than ever. Our led horses, rendered half frantic, would dart first on one side of us, then on the other, sometimes come charging up to rub themselves against the ridden horse, who, rendered steadier by the rein, was of friendly assistance for this purpose—then again, rolling upon the ground and jerking back, or pulling forward, until our arms were nearly dislocated, such is a faint picture of our situation, under circumstances.

Arrived on the banks of the Blue. (The streams all have appropriate names in this country, as for instance, the Boggy, whose peculiarities I have described; the Brushy, whose banks are tangled almost impassably, with briars and brambles, and the Blue, whose waters are a deep blue, from running over a bed of soft blue limestone and clay). My companion plead his inability to swim, as a reason for not taking the lead in crossing, so I was obliged to precede.

All would have gone well, had not my horse commenced floundering the moment his feet touched the soft clay at the bottom. In we went up to the neck, and whilst struggling to keep heads above water, what should I hear but a stanza of the Blue Moselle, quietly hummed by the imperturbable individual on the bank. With a hearty expletive, denouncing all sentiment, and particularly at such a time, I was fain to leave him to his fate, but philanthropy, getting the better of temper, I re-crossed and piloted the way to the " terra firma" of the most beautiful prairie we had yet crossed,—the prairie, upon the outer edge of which stands Fort Washita, where we arrived at sundown, sore, sunburnt and fatigued, to experience all the comfort and pleasure, which unaffected and disinterested hospitality could offer and accomplish.

CHAPTER IV.

STAY AT FORT WASHITA.

Description of the Post.—Pleasant stay among our friends.—Fossiliferous Remains.—Prairie, ancient bed of the ocean.—Prairie Flowers.—Timber through the country.—Indians met with.—Soil of the Choctaw and Chickasaw Reserves. Remarks upon the Natives.—Territorial Bill.—Captain leaves on 22d with part of the Train.

JUNE 15th to 29th.—This post, established about twelve years since, was garrisoned by one company of the seventh infantry, commanded by Major Holmes, and one company of the fourth artillery, commanded by Major Hunt; Major Holmes commanding the post. Plain, but comfortable quarters, stand upon the brow of a hill, commanding a fine view of the plain. For ten miles, this rich, green velvet carpet is spread out, spangled with flowers of every hue, and interspersed with groves of timber. A little babbling brook meanders through the green sward at the foot of the hill, the whole forming a scene of picturesque beauty, compensating in some measure for the isolation from society and the daily peril concomitant to a frontier life.

We enjoyed the hospitalities of our friend, S. HUMES, whose heart is as open as the prairie around him, and our time passed pleasantly and quickly, roaming through the prairie and exploring the palaeontological remains in the vicinity, amongst which *the indefatigable doctor* fairly revelled. Our friends got up many little social soirees for us and we were also enlivened by a wedding. One of the fair garrison belles, leaving parents and friends, cast in her lot with a young subaltern of infantry, who, after a four years' absence upon the frontier, returned to the States a Benedict; long may he and his fair bride enjoy the sweets of the faith pledged beneath the harvest moon, in the midst of Nature's choicest beauties.

Poorly paid, and worse equipped, the soldiers of our republic never can receive too high a mete of praise for the choice that decided and the energy which marks their profession.

Isolated from home and the world, they carry with them into these solitudes, refinements the result of well trained habits and education, and moving in a sphere, hallowed by feminine grace, beauty, and accomplishments, reality becomes romance, though the rose is well armed with thorns.

The country around Fort Washita bears unmistakeable evidences that, at a remote period, old ocean's surges rolled in all their might and majesty over these vast plains.

Hitherto, the idea that they were once the ancient bed of the ocean, appeared to me to be a very plausible theory, but, " experientia docet," no fact can be more fully established.

Our explorations developed every water-course, hill side and ravine to be filled with fossiliferous remains. The *indefatigable doctor* was busy from early dawn to dewy eve with hammer and specimen bag, and his cabinet now contains fossil sea eggs, fossil oysters, scollops, clams, and other marine shells, whilst in the soft limestone we found the ammonite and the nautilus (extinct marine crustacea), some of the former as large as a cart-wheel.

A suggestion has been made, that the days of Noah and the Flood will explain these deposits, but the depth of the strata and the size of the specimens found, prove revolving years of submersion and procreation. Some of the strata were fifty feet perpendicular, with numerous specimens thickly embedded from bottom to top.

What food for thought! Over a spot, now redolent with the perfume, and gay with the hues of sweet flowers, and teeming with insect and animal life, once rolled the mighty wave, sported the monsters of the deep, and roared the tempest in its irresistible might!

How ancient, then, must be this universal system—how far exceeding all the bounds set to it ; its history is as unfathomable as that of the Being who formed, and now guides and directs it ! Truly, at sight of nature's wonders, man sinks into puny insignificance.

I have frequently alluded to the beauty and variety of the prairie flowers. It is a rich treat to roam amongst them. Throughout our march we found in profusion flowers which, in the North and East, are cultivated with great care as ornaments for the drawing-room or conservatory. The Texas plume—a gorgeous flower of a brilliant scarlet—the red and white rose, the prairie pink, the verbena, the marygold of many varieties, the convolvulus, the ranunculus, the sensitive and other liguminous plants, the flag, the sunflower and the wild pea—all luxuriant in growth and brilliant in colour—all bloom here together, and though " wasting their sweetness upon the desert air," still, as the occasional tourists wander among them, they stand the fragrant evidence of creative power, hallowing the scene and raising the thoughts from nature up to nature's God.

The timber found in the country passed through is the cottonwood, black jack, post oak, pecan, pride of China, and the " bois d'arc," or Osage orange, which occurs first at Boggy. The wood of this tree is the hardest and toughest known. It is used by the Indians for making their bows, (hence its name,) is very close grained, and of a deep-yellow colour. It is also used for hedges. A very fine and lasting dye is also extracted from it. The foliage is very thick, leaf small and of a very deep-green, making it a handsome addition to the forest. It bears also a very large apple, which contains the seed, and which, when fully ripe, is a deep orange colour.

The pecan, is very useful for mechanical purposes, as it can be split into very thin laths, and is very pliable. We also found some hickory and white oak, but very rare.

Although the soil is in general a black loam and very rich, the timber is short, except the cottonwood.

The soil is well adapted for corn—the only thing the Indians raise—and vegetables, evidenced by the strength and luxuriance of the sun-flower, a plant which always flourishes best in a locality suitable for these crops.

During our stay, many Indians came in to trade at the sutler's store. They were Caddos, Chickasaws and Witchitas, a dirty, squalid and uninteresting set.

A party of Kickapoos also passed one morning, with pack-mules. They were on their way down to Red River to barter for whiskey, the bane of the red man, but which he will have, despite of law and at the risk of starvation, a melancholy depravity, to our shame be it said, entailed upon him by the white man, against which no curse can be too loud or too bitter, no effort too strenuously exerted to eradicate.

An old Chickasaw chief came in one evening, with three of his negroes, who had been kidnapped.

He related to us a singular incident connected with this affair. These negroes were kidnapped during his absence from home, and upon following them up, with a chosen party, armed to the teeth, and prepared for any emergency, he overtook them and found that the kidnapper had just died suddenly by the road-side, so that his property was recovered without any resort to knives or pistols, the usual "argumentum ad hominem" in this country.

We had now passed one hundred and eighty miles through the Choctaw and Chickasaw Reserve, as fertile a country as ever the light of day rested upon, and yet every days' experience and observation had only served to increase my feelings of depreciation of the character and habits of the natives, and my regret that so much of such fine land should be left to lie idle and unworked. Why the government should not have limited these people to a tract much smaller, and even then more than they can or will cultivate is to me a mystery. Not one-sixteenth part of it will ever be brought under cultivation, under the present system.

Climate, and every natural advantage here only serve to foster the natural indolence and distaste for all useful exertion, inherent in the Indian.

It is true, many of the natives are rich in this world's goods; it is not, however, owing to their exertions, but is the effect of the force of circumstances.

With this rich domain, inviting cultivation, and which yields tenfold for the smallest amount of cultivation from the tiller; with a market at their very doors—for this is and will be for years the main route for emigrants—and daily inquiry made for corn and fodder, which they cannot supply, they are content to live neglectful of the golden opportunity, scarcely raising enough for their own wants, and not even varying their own home-fare with an occasional potatoe or a turnip; indeed, they raise no vegetables of any kind.

Their cattle and horses roam through the luxuriant pastures, which nature clothes in verdure and life, winter and summer, uncared for, except to be driven up and branded when necessary; their hogs subsist upon the mast, and with the corn, supply their eternal diet of hog and hominy. Thus, their horses and cattle supply their hoard; their hogs and corn—the one fed from nature's bounty, the other, raised by the sweat of their slaves, in quantity sufficient to keep them from starvation—are their food; and the Indian can mount his pony and gallop whooping through the prairie, lounge dozing about his log hut, or taking his rifle, stroll listlessly about the country; in short, do any thing but work; that is a word not known in his vocabulary.

Nor does their country supply only the necessaries of life; the sumach grows in abundance and is prepared from the stalk almost in an instant.

Whilst in camp one evening during our march, I observed two Indians ride up and dismount. One of them stooped down, pulled something from under his horse's feet, and walking to the camp fire, held it over the flame. Prompted by curiosity, I went over and found him preparing *sumach for his evening's smoke.* He had pulled a bunch of the green branches of the plant, and now held them in the flame just far enough and long enough, to singe and curl them; he then rubbed them in his hands, filled his pipe, lit it, and, mounting, was gone, the whole process not detaining him five minutes.

Thus, even the luxuries of life are supplied by the same bountiful hand, and "dolce far niente" made as perfect, as imagination can conceive, or the Indian's capacity enjoy.

Even the few improvements in culinary utensils, and facilities for preparing food for cooking, are not taken advantage of. The old log burnt hollow at one end, and the rude pestle, still hold their place; the hand-mill, as old as the patriarchs, graces the chimney side, and a pot or two and an earthen jar make up the complement.

So lived their forefathers, and that their ghosts may not revisit and rebuke any innovation, the Indian world must stand still.

The style of building among this people is peculiar; two square pens are put up with logs, and roofed or thatched. The space between the pens is covered in and serves for eating-place and depository of harness, saddles and bridles, &c. A door is cut in each pen, facing the passage. They have no windows, the door admitting all the light used. This style is called *two pens and a passage*, and is, in fact, only a shelter for the family from bad weather, for of furniture they have but little, and that of the rudest and most uncomfortable kind.

These buildings are stuck (almost invariably) upon the road; no neat door yard, with a substantial fence and neat gate, encloses them; no flower or vegetable garden is seen, but the ornamental figure of a half-starved hog, grunts lazily on one side, and a pack of miserable curs lounge on the other, the whole presenting an untidy picture of squalid discomfort, which even its temporary appearance cannot deceive.

Their present code of laws, if strictly enforced, would secure all the safety to life and property necessary, but

either from indolence or inefficiency law is comparatively
a dead letter among them.

In the space of six weeks, this season, no less than five
murders were committed, and yet we met two of the crimi-
nals at large. and taken by the hand as usual.

The stringent law against the introduction of whiskey
may occasionally be enforced, but when it is, it is because
the facts are too palpable to allow of any escape.

The Bible, and the missionary, have failed to eradicate
their veneration for and superstitious belief in the medicine
man.

At different points on our road we were witnesses to
the absurd pow-wow and ridiculous incantation of these
swindlers.

Near the hut where lies the patient, they erect a pole,
from the top of which flaunts gay ribbons and pieces of gay
cloth. At the foot of the pole stands a frame, to which is
attached a bale of muslin or woolen cloth, ribbons, &c.,
and the door of the hut is festooned with ribbons and
colored cloth.

The mighty medicine man goes through with his mum-
meries, and leaves, taking the precaution to take with him,
as perquisites, all the cloth, ribbons, &c., which have been
used, and according to his wants, of muslin, woolen or rib-
bon, so will be the quantity required, and the quality of
these infallible antidotes to the disease to be cured. What
a commentary upon a people having all the advantages of

the civilization and enlightenment of the nineteenth century !

A bill has been introduced into Congress, by the young and talented Senator from Arkansas, to organize a territorial government, which, sanctioning the privilege of purchase in, and settlement upon, the Reserves, by the white population from the States, would soon change the face of affairs for the better, for what clearer proof is necessary of the inefficiency of the pure blooded native to manage in a civilized community, than the fact, that in almost every instance, the leading men in these tribes are either half-breeds, or have a tincture of white blood in their veins.

The Senator has displayed the highest grade of philanthropy and sagacity by his efforts in this cause, and if successful, will not only elevate and retrieve the Indian character from aspersion, but relieve the general government from a heavy burden of imputation of wrong and injustice, under which it now labors.

Two views are to be taken of the savage state. Either it is a state of degradation from original greatness, or else the natural condition of man. If the former, it may be restored ; if the latter, it may be improved.

That nations may decline in civilization, is evidenced in the degraded condition of the nomadic hordes that roam the vast plains of the East, descendants of a people who built the greatest cities of their time, but that they may be improved, is a cardinal principle of philanthropy.

The modern Englishman is as far removed in civilization from his ancestor, the savage Briton, clothed in skins and dwelling in huts, as the American from the Indian, or as the humanized condition of the African race among us differs from the brutal condition of the negro in Guinea; and if mere contact with civilization can produce such results, what would not a systematic effort effect, when brought to bear upon a race degraded from either of the causes named.

The policy of our government has been practically to deny the capacity of the Indians for civilization, by compelling them to hold their lands in common, and not in severalty, depriving them of the power of alienation, thereby creating no necessity for self-reliance and individual effort.

I know that some of our wisest statesmen, and men of philanthropic and benevolent natures, have pronounced this the most merciful policy, and that intelligent whitemen, who have had opportunities of studying the Indian character, either in an official capacity or as missionaries, or as traders, have pronounced civilization to be so repugnant to the native that he will not submit to its wholesome restraints, and hence that the phrase, "Injun will be Injun," has become trite, yet I contend that the Indian never can be elevated but by his individual effort, and that thrift, prudence, and discipline of character, the real elements of civilization, can never be attained until he has to depend upon himself, a result never to be arrived at so long as his lands are held in common.

That some would fall a prey to the speculator and become still lower in the scale of degradation, must be expected ; but they would be but a minority, and not to be considered in the ultimate benefits, and situated as we are towards the red man, it is our duty—as it should be our earnest desire and pleasure—to atone for his wrongs by affording him every reasonable facility for his possible improvement.

My sympathies are with the aborigines, and I cannot better express them than by advocating, with voice and pen, a measure which seems to me to be fraught with more ultimate good results for them than any heretofore promulged by our statesmen.　Let them once be involved in common interests with white men, and a new impulse would be given to them. They would substitute practical life for sensual existence, accumulate wealth where they now barely scratch out a support, and, instead of degraded peasants, would become wealthy agriculturists.

It is not the ability that the Indian wants, it is example, and to be brought daily into contact with the results of well directed industry, both of body and mind.　This would be effected by the bill proposed, and which no well-wisher of the Indian can for a moment oppose.

Though the days of Tahmehund and Logan, of Tecumseh and Red Jacket, have long passed away, and though their virtues, energies and moral worth live but in history, still many scions of the stock may arise to kindle anew the burning fires of their eloquence and reflect new splendor upon ancient aboriginal renown. Let us cherish the hope, that ere long the Indian representative may be found occupying his seat in our national legislature, to advocate his own cause and secure his rights from oppression.

I was not surprised in conversing with many of the old men of the tribes, on the subject of this bill, to find them all of one opinion.

They are strongly opposed to it, and wind up all their conversations with the same conclusion, viz., that it is a scheme of the white man to dispossess them of their lands. They say, " We got land now, we keep him ; white man come, all is gone."

This idea is a necessary consequence of their inherent distrust of our race. At heart they hate us, and are only kept apparent friends by either fear or self-interest.

The young men who have had some advantages of education, and mingled more with the population of the States, are more favourably disposed to the newly proposed arrangement, a fact which is acknowledged by the old men with much bitterness, and either denounced as treason or as a scheme to rise in power and influence in the tribes.

I took my leave of this fair spot in earth's garden with mingled feelings of regret and pity—regret, that so much beauty and fertility was wasted upon indolence and obtuseness; pity, to find all but the spirit of man divine.

Our train arrived on the twenty-second, and on the twenty-sixth the Captain, having concluded all arrangements, left with part of it, intending to cross Red River and wait for the arrival of the military escort and the rest of our wagons, &c., at the Lower Cross-Timbers.

CHAPTER V.

FORT WASHITA TO LOWER CROSS TIMBERS.

Leave the Fort.—Military escort.—Adventure with a Chickasaw.—Arrive at Red
River.—Scenes at the Ferry.—Town of Preston.—Desperate fight.—Description
of soil, &c.—Cross Big Mineral.—Basin Spring.—Distances on Plains deceptive.—Arrive at Lower Cross Timbers.

JUNE 29th.—At noon to-day we left our comfortable quarters at our friend S. H——'s, and bidding adieu to Washita,
with its green plains, noble hearts and bright faces, we entered
the timber, skirting the plain on the south-east, and commenced our long journey to unexplored Texas.

Our military escort, which arrived on the twenty-eighth,
consisted of forty non-commissioned officers and men, from
the seventh Regiment of infantry, commanded by Lieutenants
P——e and C——n of that regiment.

The command was a mixed one of Americans, Germans and
Irish, a fine body of men, and as they had all volunteered for
the expedition, we flattered ourselves that, should we get into
a fight, we should have good material to depend upon.

The afternoon was oppressively hot, so we made but a short
march, and on coming into camp found two-thirds of the command " hors de combat," from indulging too freely in whiskey,
where obtained no one could tell, but the fact spoke for
itself.

To add to our discomfort, a party of drunken Indians came howling and yelling around camp, so that the night passed in restlessness and apprehensions for the morrow.

It is almost invariably the case, when commencing a march, that the common soldier must have a frolic; whether to drown regret at leaving his barracks, or in drinking farewell with his friends, or that he takes advantage of whiskey depots on his route, cannot be told; most probably each of the three reasons has its weight, and the latter, perhaps, the weightiest of all.

It is not a common drunk, either, that he indulges in, but one that, unless he gets into the hands of the guard, leaves him stripped of accoutrements, and almost of clothes, absorbing months of his scanty pay in an afternoon's debauch.

The most watchful care, on the part of his officer, fails to prevent this evil, and the only thing that can be done is to make the offender suffer the penalty of his offence.

Some did not get into camp at all, and canteens, belts, and even muskets, were strewed along, just where recklessness or oblivion overtook the Bacchanal, to be picked up if it might so happen, if not, to be charged against his score on pay day.

Captain Whiskey's account of profit and loss, had a long list on the debit side for this day's work; we were fortunate however, in not having a mutiny to cap the climax.

During the evening a young Chickasaw—a very fine specimen of the Indian—came into our camp and asked for whiskey. He was quite drunk at the time, and we declined giving him any stimulant whatever. Very soon after he took a fancy to a calico shirt I wore, and offered a gaily trimmed hunting shirt in exchange. I gave him the shirt, and in a short time he jumped up suddenly to leave. Springing on his horse, we then observed that he had appropriated a knife belonging to Lieutenant P——e, and a buckskin coat belonging to our servant. We immediately charged him with the theft, when he flew into a terrible rage, swearing vengeance and heaping imprecations upon us. We advanced upon him in a quiet, but determined manner, when he threw down the coat, but galloped off with the knife, swearing bitterly all the while, and gesticulating violently as far as we could see him. We kept a good look out for him, but saw no more of him, though we learned in the morning, that he was one of the party who made the night hideous by their howls and yells around camp.

June 30th.—Our march to day was very dull and uninteresting, our road at first, running over a succession of rough, steep hills, covered with low oaks; the weather oppressively hot, and the men suffering from their debauch.

Five miles brought us to a very wide prairie, which we crossed, admiring the beautiful flowers, as usual, and every moment starting quails or grouse from their hiding places in the rich grass.

This prairie was almost a level plain, extending to the horizon, and consequently not so attractive a view as those previously seen.

After leaving it, we entered the timber, which lined the road all the way to Red River, and passing many Indian farms, all looking alike—to describe one is to describe all—we encamped upon the skirt of Red River bottom early in the afternoon, to allow the stragglers to come in, and to prepare for crossing the stream in the morning. Soon the *guard-house*—a sunny spot on the hill-side, where they could boil at leisure—was filled with delinquents; and evening parade presented a funny farce, of bloody noses, torn clothes, and lame excuses, ending by bringing some ropes into requisition, and tying several of the transgressors to trees, to spend the night among gnats, musquitoes and other serenaders, which abounded in any quantity, a romantic commencement to a long, hot, and perilous march.

July 1st.—One would have supposed that the experience of the two last days would have been a sufficient lesson to our gallant sons of Mars, but the sequel of this day will prove the contrary.

We left camp at sunrise, and marching two miles through the low, sandy bottom, thickly wooded with cottonwood trees, with their limbs beautifully festooned with the trumpet creeper, in full bloom, we arrived on the shores of Red River, which we were obliged to cross by ferry boat, causing considerable delay from our numbers, and the weight of our wagons.

We found ("en bivouac," upon the high bank), a party of Seminole Indians, men, women, and children, who had come

a distance of one hundred and fifty miles, through the
Reserve, to purchase whiskey on the opposite, or Texas shore
of the river.

They were engaged in crossing it over in five gallon kegs.
These they afterwards slung on their pack-horses in a netting
made of raw hide. About fifty gallons were already piled
upon the bank in kegs, and more arriving every hour or two.

The women were quite the most industrious of the party,
although assisting in procuring the cause of most of the
brutal treatment they receive from their husbands.

Though not low enough to be fordable, the water was still
low enough to cause much trouble in getting the large flat up
to the bank, so, being impatient to cross, I stepped into a
skiff, which held Indians and empty kegs, and was soon over.

On the way, I incidentally asked the ferryman, what he
charged for this service, when to my surprise he replied,
" Why, them as buys whiskey we don't charge nothin'; them
as dos'nt, it's a bit." Proving a concert of action between
himself and the rum-seller, who can afford to pay well for
every votary brought to his shrine, as he sells the fiery stuff
at *two dollars* per gallon, it costing him *fifteen cents.*

There is no means, at present, of preventing this traffic,
the general government having no jurisdiction upon the
Texas shore. All that can be done, is for the Light Horse
to be vigilant and firm in the execution of the law.

The first person I met on landing, was the captain of the
troop, a young Chickasaw, son of a chief.

He was waiting patiently until the whole purchase should be crossed over into the Reserve, when he followed with his men, and promptly destroyed it all, amounting in value paid to one hundred and forty dollars. May he continue vigilant in this good cause, and perhaps, examples made, and the penalties suffered, may, in time, arrest this horrible evil.

The town of Preston, from which all this misery for the Red man emanates, is a collection of low groggeries and a few stores, lining the high bluff bank of the river.

It is notorious as the scene of some most cold-blooded and cruel murders, committed in open day, and with—up to that time—perfect impunity. This, together with the detestable traffic I have just alluded to, has brought such a stigma upon the place, that the very name is sufficient for all that is ruthless and vicious.

Whether our men had saved some drams from the old stock, or whether they procured a new supply from the Seminoles, we knew not, but to our surprise and dissatisfaction, they began to get noisy and uproarious before leaving the shores of the nation, and by the time that, with the most strenuous exertions on the part of the officers and the few sober men in the command, our heavy train and oxen were ferried over, insubordination was rife in the ranks.

So soon as they could be formed upon the Texas shore, the officers marched them rapidly through the village, but it being late in the afternoon, and the weather very hot, they concluded to make but a short march, and, leaving the command in charge of the serjeant, preceded a short distance to search for good camping ground.

Immediately, a scene of brutal and bloody confusion commenced, which left indelible marks, not only on our memories, but upon the heads and limbs of the drunken actors in it.

Scarcely had we reached a good camping spot, when a man came up, breathless, saying, that murder had been committed; and before the officer in command could gallop to the battle ground, two men came in, one, so completely bathed in blood, that but for his oaths, imprecations, and gesticulations, he would have been taken for any thing else than a human being,

These men were both Irishmen, who had long been inimical, and meeting during the general melee, both heated with liquor, and one over elated from having just come off champion in a single combat, the desperate manner in which they fought, was evidenced by the injuries received.

Upon examination, one was found to have received twenty-two incised wounds upon the head, neck, face and arms, one finger cut off, terribly bruised about the body, and a stab in the back, seven inches long, and an inch and a quarter deep, yet, like a wild beast, he wallowed in his gore, and with the strength of a lion, strove again and again, to reach his antagonist, who, with a wound from a bayonet, in the left breast, lay panting for breath and vomiting blood, a few

7*

yards off. Others were badly bruised and beaten, and in fact, the major part of the command were in a state unfitting them for discipline, or even punishment.

Thus ended our dreams of a quiet march for the rest of our journey. We had hoped, that the examples made before, would have had a salutary effect, but behold, some of the very men who had transgressed and been punished, now worse than ever, whilst to crown all, the chief non-commissioned officer was one of the principals in the bloodiest affray, and now lay completely "hors de combat."

What a life does a subaltern of infantry lead! It is all very pretty to write on paper, and to talk of the chivalry and romance of a soldier's life, of the tented field, the glittering review, or the charging squadron, but when we come to the realities, (as experienced in our service,) of a young lieutenant, with no protection but his nerves and individual dexterity in arms, no guide but his sense of duty, sent out upon a lonely prairie, to govern a company of men, formed of every nation almost under the sun; men naturally brutal and vicious when sober, worse than brutes when drunk; aware that but little compromise will be made, or consideration of circumstances taken count of, should disaster occur; knowing, too, that his duty is done at the risk of health and life, and for a pittance of pay as inadequate as it is ungenerous, it seems to me, that he who can find romance in such a life must draw largely upon his imagination.

The officers commanding this escort were both very young men, but watchful, energetic, and determined; and it is to these traits of character that we were indebted for no greater disaster, as in the preservation of discipline they were supported but by two or three worthy exceptions among the men. We camped about six miles from Preston, and spent a very uncomfortable night.

From Fort Washita to Red river, the soil is loam, with ridges of limestone. The timber, oak and pecan, with occasional bois d'arc and cottonwood. The river takes its name from the colour of its water, which is a dark maroon, full of sediment, and very unpalatable

The Texas shore is very bold, presenting a stratification of red clay and white sand, giving a striking and very peculiar appearance in the distance, like chalk cliffs.

The stream is but seldom in good boating order, rapid, and full of shifting shoals, making a very tedious ferriage.

Whilst we were crossing, a herd of about twelve hundred wild cattle were driven into the river from the Texas shore, to swim them over into the Nation.

Taking the course of the stream, they swam down some distance, so that the whole herd was in the water at the same time, presenting a most singular appearance, with their long, sharp pointed horns and taper heads, only seen above the surface.

A herd of one hundred and fifty mustang mares was also driven across.

These mares were taken wild on the plains, and were intended for the breeding of mules in Missouri.

Having read many descriptions, and seen drawings of the noble horse in his native wilds, what was my surprise to find a poor, miserable, spindle-shanked, puny stock, not one of which I would accept as a gift (particularly if good points were the object), and at the same time to be told that they were very excellent specimens of the breed.

I account for their degeneracy, from the unavoidable breeding in and in, which is inevitable in a wild state, and to which may be attributed the ill shape and small size of so many domesticated Indian ponies.

The mustangs have proved entirely worthless for all service, wherever the experiment has been tried, very vicious, and of no powers of endurance on the road.

This experiment of mule raising, may be successful, but I should doubt it very much; the stubbornness of the ass, and the viciousness of the mustang, not being the proper ingredients for serviceable domestic stock.

July 2d.—Hospital duties, and the necessity of providing some means of transportation for the wounded of yesterday, (our ambulance having gone on with the Captain), detained us until a late hour this morning.

The non-commissioned officer, either from real suffering, or shame that he had set so bad an example, was in an apparently very distressed state, but after a time, a reclining place was found for him in one of the wagons. The rest marched with the command, an instance of power of endurance in the one so badly wounded, seldom to be met with, his loss of blood, and the intense heat of the weather considered. Before leaving, a laughable incident occurred.

A man (who had shone conspicuous in the revel and fight) came up to the Doctor, with both his eyes bunged shut.

"Doctor," says he, in a rich brogue, "am I fornint ye, for divil a bit can I see ounly daylight. Won't ye plaze and cut me eyes open, for how do yees expict a blind man till travil an this a strange counthry. Cut thim open, Doctor dear; sure I'll niver flinch, and if I hed thim opin I could see as will as ony man in the Company;" a fact which the Doctor did not dispute, but declined the operation, so tied on a pony, and it led by the guard, poor Pat had to put up with "*ounly daylight*" for that day at least.

Noon found us crossing the Big Mineral, a limestone stream running through a rich bottom, thickly grown up with large cotton wood, honey locust, overcup, and other heavy timber, besides plenty of the bois d'arc. The overcup is a species of oak, bearing an acorn as large as a hen's egg. The tree is very tall and straight, making excellent timber for building purposes.

After leaving Preston, we entered upon the vast plains, which stretching to the Cross Timbers, gave us a foretaste of our home, and the seat of our labors for many weeks.

From this point, there is but a house here and there, and

the little village of Gainesville, until we reach the Upper Cross Timbers, and then adieu to all outward signs of civilization.

Early in the afternoon, we stopped at the *Basin Spring*, a perfect fairy bath tub, and fatigued with the scenes of the past three days, overcome by the intense heat, and almost famished with thirst, but above all, enamored with the place, we determined to encamp for the night.

An apparently dry ravine ran at right angles to our course, on traversing which, we came suddenly upon a series of ledges of limestone rock, arranged like stairs.

Over these, the water trickled, and was caught in a basin, worn by time and the action of the water, about three feet deep, and five in diameter, and so pellucid, that the smallest article might be seen on the bottom.

After the muddy waters of Red River, and the stagnant pools of the prairies, what wonder that we hailed this fountain with delight, drank copious draughts, laved in its cool refreshing bosom, and poured out libations to the Naiad of the Spring. We did all this, aye, more, for we treated her to a serenade, the first we had felt any spirits for since leaving Fort Washita; and cooled, calmed and refreshed, an early hour found us wrapped in that slumber which only the tired man can really enjoy.

July 3d.—Daylight found us bidding adieu to the Nymphs of the fountain, and entering upon the last large prairie we crossed before reaching the Cross Timbers.

After marching three miles, we came to a house nestled in a clump of trees, in the open prairie.

We found, after making inquiries here, how deceptive distances are on these plains.

The man had never been beyond his house, in the direction we were travelling, and in reply to our inquiry, how far it was to the timber, which was in sight, and where we expected to join Captain Marcy, he said, "about three miles," and truly it did not seem farther, but it was eight miles, two hours' travel before we reached the outskirts, and three miles farther we found the Captain encamped in a very cozy skirting of timber by the roadside.

The eye is deceived quite as much on the plains as on the water; the long stretches of prairie, although undulating, present no object so prominent as the belt of timber which bounds them, so that the eye rests at once upon this, skipping over the intermediate space and shortening the distance just in proportion as the ground is level or broken.

These Cross Timbers are a very singular growth. The one we had now entered is called the Lower Cross Timbers, and is about six miles wide; then eighteen miles from the outer edge of this one, we should enter the Upper and larger. They extend almost due north and south, from the Canadian to the Brazos. The timber is a short, stunted oak, not growing in a continuous forest, but interspersed with open glades, plateaus, and vistas of prairie scenery, which give a very picturesque and pleasing variety.

Thus far from Washita I had missed the flowers. A few were still left, but they had lost the charm of profusion and luxuriance.

It was to be sure getting late in the season, and I must expect that soon these prairie gems would vanish entirely from our sight, but the thought caused me much regret; there was such a home feeling about them, it was like missing "the old familiar faces."

I found no new varieties to add to those already collected and described, except a convolvulus, and a species of lauristinus, of both of which I obtained specimens.

The Captain having concluded to dispense with one of the teams, and send it back to Washita, the afternoon was spent in dispatching by this unexpected opportunity, letters to our far off friends and home, when, after a pleasant bath in a little stream below camp, we resigned ourselves to our blankets for the night.

CHAPTER VI.

LOWER CROSS TIMBERS TO UPPER CROSS TIMBERS.

Camp on Elm Fork of Trinity.—Independence day.—Arrival of Indian hunters.—
Remarks on the Delawares.—Arrival at Gainesville.—Description of Tornado.—
Funny scene in Gainesville.—Last house in Texas.—Parlance of the settlers.—
Camp on the Trinity.—Night march.—Manner of tracking horses by the
Indians.—First rattlesnake killed.—Arrival at Upper Cross Timbers.

July 4th.—Independence day found us on the march just as day dawned, and soon leaving the timber, we entered upon a broken country, conisting of ridges of sand and limestone, interspersed with small prairies and small strips of timber, principally black jack, until we emerged upon and crossed Elm Fork of the Trinity, where, on account of the intense heat, Captain Marcy determined to halt and encamp, thereafter, intending to march by moonlight, until we reached the Grand Prairie.

This stream runs over a bed of reddish limestone, very full of fossils, principally the oyster and the periwinkle, and winding through an extensive prairie, offered a very pretty camp, whereat to spend our national holiday.

Soon the tents were pitched, and a ration of grog issued to the men, whilst our mess indulged in a bumper of claret, and some excellent cake, presented us by the old cook at Washita.   This, with the Star Spangled Banner, Hail

8

Columbia, and Yankee Doodle, of course, roared out at the top of not the weakest lungs, constituted our celebration, our echoes bringing into camp an old squatter, who, roused from his solitude by such vociferous republicanism, came to ascertain the meaning of the invasion. His curiosity was gratified to our gain, as we procured from him some excellent butter, at the moderate rate of a bit a pound, a rich treat in camp.

During the afternoon, we were agreeably surprised by the arrival of John Wagon, and John Jackson, our two Delaware hunters and guides.

The manner and the certainty with which they found us, shows how invaluable this race of men is for such service.

Whilst we lay at Washita, Captain Marcy visited Fort Arbuckle, and left word with Big Beaver—a famous Delaware—to procure him hunters and guides. He could not procure them in time to join us at Washita, but ascertaining our route, and time of departure, these men took a straight course across the country, guided by the stars, swimming Red River, and other intervening streams, subsisting on cold flour,* and what game they met with, and struck our camp— one hundred and ninety miles from Fort Arbuckle—on the afternoon of the fourth day, as accurately as though they had

---

* Cold flour is a preparation of corn. It is first parched, then pounded and according to taste, a little sugar mixed with it. A handful of this will make a int of gruel, upon which a man can subsist for twenty-four hours.

only been making an excursion in the neighbourhood, and came in as unconcerned as only an Indian can be.

They were paid—for their services during our expedition—one dollar and a half a day, and one ration, besides having transportation for the skins of deer, &c., that they might kill.

We congratulated ourselves on the prospect of now having plenty of game, (as they are famous hunters,) which would be a delightful change from salt provisions in such hot weather.

The Delawares and Shawnees are among Indians, what the Jews are among Christians.

Coming originally from the shores of the Delaware River, they are scattered thoughout the South and West, though their principal settlement is on Caw River, in Missouri.

Wherever they are found, they preserve the same character for truth, honesty, and intelligence, and are ever ready, at a moment's warning, to take service, as hunters, guides, or interpreters, and travel off hundreds of miles from home.

They serve entirely in these capacities, and are universally known and esteemed by travellers in our wild territories, in fact, it is almost impossible to get any other Indians to perform these duties; they are either too selfish, too lazy, or too ignorant, and when applied for, always make the same reply, "Delaware he do dat, may be so you get him."

We tried the experiment—as a matter of curiosity—when in the Choctaw and Chickasaw country, but to no purpose. They all knew the capabilities of the Delawares, and always ended by suggesting them. They are a noble race, very athletic, but short in stature.

It is a religious principle with them never to run from the foe, a fact which their enemies attribute to a funny cause, viz., the shortness of their legs, they say "Delaware can't run, he got short leg, must stand and fight heap."

One of their superstitions is, that the Great Spirit in the shape of a huge eagle hovers over them. When pleased, he appears in the clouds, and occasionally drops a feather. When angry, he rises out of sight, and speaks in thunder. The feather is supposed to render the wearer invulnerable.

The Delawares and Shawnees assimilate and intermarry. We expected an addition of three Delawares and a Shawnee, at Fort Belknap, thus making our Indian corps complete, and formidable.

Sun down, found the camp all bustle, preparatory to a night march, and ere the harvest moon showed her calm pale face, we were on the road to Gainesville, where we arrived in two hours.

This collection of five or six log cabins, dignified with the name of a town, was rendered celebrated in the annals of storms by a most terrific tornado, which occurred here on the twenty-eighth of May, (the same whose ravages I before remarked upon in the Choctaw Nation), the traces of which, had they not come under my observation, too palpably to be mistaken, I should have put down in the same category with the Munchausen stories.

About dark, on the day mentioned, this storm arose, and passing over the country in a vein a mile wide, left marks of its ravages, which were as indelible as they were destructive.

The motion of the tornado was undulatory, evidenced by the manner in which every thing it came in contact with was treated; as for instance, a very heavy ox wagon was taken up and carried a quarter of a mile, where it stuck in the ground to the axletree; taken up again, it was carried several hundred yards farther, and there the wheels were twisted off, and a tire broken and twisted into several pieces.

Fences were blown off, driven into the ground, broken off, and again blown a long distance.

Two women were taken up and blown three-quarters of a mile, impinging three times against the ground in their terrific flight.

A horse was blown into a tree, where it happened to catch by its fore-leg and shoulder; these were torn from the body and were still hanging there, the balance of the carcase lying in a field full a-quarter of a mile off.

A sheep was blown into the top of a high tree, where we saw it as we passed.

The strata of wind seems also to have been about ten feet from the ground, rising and falling, as the trees in its course were broken off in a manner clearly so to indicate. One house, also, was blown down to the foundations, whilst another, beyond and in a line with it, had the roof taken off. In short, the whole scene indicated the result of great and inconceivable power exerted, fortunately attended with but little loss of life and limb.

The same tornado destroyed the buildings and the beautiful parade at Fort Towson, one hundred and forty miles distant, creating a most singular coincidence, viz.: orders had just been received to abandon the post, and remove the troops, &c., to Fort Arbuckle; these were nearly executed, when the tornado occurred; so that, in the same week, it was abandoned by government and also by heaven, and is now a complete ruin.

Being considerably in advance of the train, P——e and myself went to a small store to make some purchases, when a laughable incident occurred.

On our way to the store, we met a man with but one leg, who proved to be the proprietor.

P——e, in conversation, asked him how he lost his leg; he told us, and proved to be a jolly fellow.

An article we wanted not being on hand, he directed us to another store near his; on going into which, what was our surprise to find its proprietor also *minus a leg*, and before we completed our purchase, our quondam acquaintance came in, when upon my remarking that two one-legged men were quite a large proportion for so small a place— " Oh," says he, " there are two more, and three of us board at the same house; I shouldn't wonder if he came in, he's here a'most every night,"—and sure enough he did (strange as it may appear), and joined in our merry laugh at so funny a coincidence.

I proposed a race for a bottle of whiskey, when, to our surprise, they assented, and started off up the road, whilst we, dying with laughter, were obliged to ride off, being behind the train some distance.

A more absurdly ridiculous sight cannot be imagined, than the six crutches and three legs scampering off in the moonlight. Long and loud were our shouts of laughter and those of our camp companions, when we related the scene, and Gainesville remains the one-legged settlement, from that date, in our memories.

In an hour, we arrived at the last house in Texas, and entering a piece of timber which crossed our road—a spur of the Cross Timbers—found it impracticable on account of the late storm, and consequently were obliged to encamp until a road could be cut through.

We retraced our steps to a clear spring, near the house, and despite musquitoes,—which abounded in thousands,—camped for the night.

During our detention, I visited the house to make purchases, if possible, of eggs, chickens, milk, &c., for our mess, and was much amused—as I had been before—at the peculiar parlance of the settlers, as for instance—"Will you sell me some eggs?" "We ha'nt got nar an eggs." "Any chickens?" "We ha'nt got nar a chickens." "Any milk?"

"We ha'nt got nary milk." These replies were given with a strong nasal twang, totally indescribable. I made out, however, at length, to get "a chickens," and returned to camp with the odd lingo still ringing in my ears.

July 5th.—Our camp proved very uncomfortable and bare of pasture, so as soon as the road was clear, we struck tents and made a short march to a fresh and grassy meadow on the banks of Elm Fork of Trinity River.

At the crossing of this stream, we made some very interesting fossiliferous collections, among the rest a nautilus, very large and an entirely new species.

During the afternoon, Wagon saddled up and was gone about half an hour, when he returned with his first deer, a fat doe.

The stream abounded in fish, among which was a new species of cat-fish of a deep jet black, several of which were added to our collection.

Preparatory to our night march, we all indulged in a delicious bath in this clear limestone water, and at sunset were off, with a thunder-storm rumbling in the east, and lighted on our way by the prairie on fire in our rear. A high wind arose just as we started, and the cook's fire being scattered, a fine effect was produced, as the night waxed older and the storm-cloud grew blacker—on one side a pillar of fire—on the other a pillar of cloud—and the wilderness between—a striking picture of the sublime, which left a deep impression upon us all.

We made a very long march and at midnight encamped upon a branch of the same stream.

July 6th.—This morning our Indians rendered us a most important service.

The fatigue of the last march had made the ostlers careless, and our horses having been loosely picketed, every horse but two was missing at daylight.

Fearful of consequences, the frightened ostlers were scouring around for hours, but unsuccessfully, when report being made to the Captain, he dispatched the Delawares, who quietly saddling up, were gone about an hour, and returned with the whole troop, besides each had shot a fat doe, so that with the one shot yesterday venison abounded in camp. The plan they pursued was to ride in a straight line to the outside of the pickets, and then make a circle completely around camp, before completing which, they struck the trail of the stray animals, and following it up soon overtook them.

The stream here was very narrow, but afforded water sufficient for our use, and a short distance above camp we found a pool large enough to bathe in, which we availed ourselves of just before starting in the evening.

A bright moon shone over us on this our last march before reaching the Upper Cross Timbers. In fine spirits our party rolled along, cracking jokes and carolling snatches of wild song, when just as we passed the brow of a hill, our harmony was checked by a rapid k-r-r-r k-r-r-r-r, rattle, rattle, rattle, and a voice exclaimed, "look out, look to your left," and sure enough, there, almost under my horse's feet and coiled ready to strike, lay an enormous diamond rattlesnake, looking ten times more deadly in the moonlight. Bang! bang! went revolvers—k-r-r-r-r, k-r-r-r-r, went the rattle—"there he goes,"—"here he is,"—"there, hit him with your ramrod,"—"ah, that will do,"—"now, bring him out." "My eyes, what a whopper! did yees iver see the like? sure we have none of sich divils in the ould country, the bloody tief; what do they make sich a ting fur ony how?" said Paddy Thompson (the same lad who had his eyes bunged in the late melee) "hould im up 'till I look at im,"—and there he hung, six feet long and eleven rattles,— "an soul, but it's mesilf 'ill kape out o' the weeds if there mony jintilmen like him there," said the same genius. This was the first large specimen we had met with. Our long boots and thick gloves were now indispensable, as *these jintle-men* are not at all trustworthy.

This Thompson was a queer specimen of the Emerald Isle. An old deserter from the British army, he was the Caleb Quotem of his company, soldier, smith, carpenter, shoemaker, poet and vocalist, but his love of whiskey kept him in the hands of the guard more than three-fourths of his time.

It was amusing, on the march, to hear him rolling out his Irish camp songs, one of which—the confounded refrain of which rings in my ears as I write—called the fate of Nell Flaherty's Drake, was a great favorite among his comrades, and even whilst blind from his fight, his voice could be heard with the richest brogue and merriest tone, as though nothing had happened.

Such is the rakish, vagabond spirit of the Irishman, which suffering cannot depress, privation cannot subdue. The soldier and laborer of the world, in the words of the old song—

> " Och, for drinkin', for fightin' or handlin' the flail,
> Whoop, the boys of ould Ireland will niver turn tail."

About nine o'clock we halted for the night near a small pond skirted with timber, and the weather being so warm, concluded to sleep " en bivouac." It was not long before the insect world made us sensible of their presence, and after enduring their attacks for a brief season, I left my blanket under the trees, and started to see how the Indians managed. They always bivouaced some distance from camp, and upon my approach I saw a sight which caused me to stop and admire.

They had divested themselves of their scanty attire, and with their blankets spread under them, sat cross-legged, erect, and perfectly motionless, looking like two bronze statues in the moonlight. It was a study for the sculptor, a moment to realize a preconceived idea of symmetry in form and grace in posture.

At this season they always sleep in the open prairie, and away from trees or underbrush. Taking the hint, I moved my quarters also out into the moonlight and enjoyed my rest, whilst my companions were slapping and scratching in the busiest manner all night.

CHAPTER VII.

UPPER CROSS TIMBERS TO LITTLE WITCHITA.

Thoughts at Sunset.—Enter the Timber.—Camp fire half way.—Old soldier
brought in.—Jackson's Adventure.—Singular Mounds.—The Delawares in
Camp.—Sunset Scene.—Arrive at Little Witchita.

July 7th.—At an early hour the Captain decided to cross
the remaining three miles of road intervening to the edge of
the Upper Cross Timbers, and encamping for the day, commence the passage early in the evening.

Soon the train was in motion, and without breakfast we
marched briskly along, snuffing the fresh air of the flowery and
dew-spangled prairie, until we reached a clear limestone spring
where tents were soon pitched and preparations made to satisfy
appetites keenly sharpened by the morning's work.

Before leaving our bivouac I caught an enormous tarantula
and a large species of wasp, which burrows in the sand and is
very venomous, as it avenged its death by stinging me, from
the effects of which my hand was lame for a week.

One of the men caught a large diamond rattlesnake, five
feet long, with eight rattles, which being unbruised I prepared
for our collection; we also caught a new species of lizard and
made some addition to our fossils.

Wagon brought in another fat doe, and Jackson brought

me a cup of his cold flour gruel to taste, which was a great
curiosity to me. It tasted like mush, and was very palatable
and cooling.

We caught several horned frogs, a species of lizard, very
nimble and curious little creatures, quite harmless, and long-
lived, even when deprived of food, one having been kept six
months unfed.

In this way the day passed pleasantly and quickly, and
sunset found us all ready to enter the timber.

The road from our camp ascended gradually over the
prairie for about a mile, when suddenly and abruptly we
found ourselves upon the brink of a steep and precipitous
descent. On either side large grassy bluffs stood like
fortifications, terrace and bastion rising one over the other,
as if to guard the entrance. Below, stretching as far as the
eye could reach, lay the apparently interminable forest of
the Cross Timbers, like a barrier, on passing which we were
to be shut out from civilization, its joys and cares, for many,
many weeks.

We all stopped involuntarily to cast a last lingering look
North, where lay all that we held most dear, and home,
sweet home, never sounded more sadly sweet than when
sung at that hour, with the last rays of a summer sunset
deepening the shadows of the battlemented mounds and
darkening the thick foliage at our feet. One look more,
one sigh, one heartfelt prayer to Heaven that we might be

9

spared to return and tell of all the wonders and beauties of nature we had seen and were to see, and we were gone.

The long twilight and the bright moon succeeding made our journey through the woods much easier than we had anticipated, though the road was much broken and the trees low, stunted and very dense.

The timber is post oak and black jack, and the soil very poor.

Though these night marches prevented our making many observations along the road, still they were very judicious, as the oxen escaped the heat, and better still, the flies, which as I before observed rendered them almost unmanageable. There is a wildness about them, also, which renders them very fascinating. To watch the shadows grow deeper and deeper, to let the fancy play and imagine a lurking foe in every thicket, or fashion a stunted tree or a bush into a panther or a wolf—then to ride in advance of the train, build a fire, and flinging oneself upon the ground, snatch a few moments sleep, or carol out some camp-fire ditty, with wolves howling in the distance, and miles of uninhabited country around, is a romance in real life, which to be enjoyed must be experienced.

Intending to pass entirely through before camping, we stopped half-way to rest the cattle, and lighting a blazing fire, our sad thoughts at sunset gave way to many a rollicksome glee and hearty joke, until the old woods rang with merriment, and the bright moon seemed to shine brighter still upon our noisy bivouac. Paddy Thompson came in to report that he had found "an ould citizen feller"—as he expressed himself—in the woods and brought him in, and—"sowl," said he, "I wouldn't ha' got him at all, only he kaughed in the grass, then I knowed it was a humin." He proved to be a poor, squalid-looking, half-clad and half-crazed creature, who had been a soldier. He was now wandering about half starved, trying to find his way to Fort Belknap. The officers told him to keep with the command, but as soon as he had supped off the contents of a haversack, he disappeared and we saw no more of him.

In an hour we were again under way, and reaching the prairie we pitched our tents, picketed our horses, and all, except the sentinels, were soon wrapt in sleep.

July 8th.—This morning Jackson was missing. He soon came in, however, and with a most lugubrious countenance, related his story of the night.

He said—"Me see de fire light, den me tink, may be so he camp here. Me take blanket, lie down, go sleep; me git up, no man is dere; may be so all gone; now is day light, me see trail, come on." This he said in reference to our camp fire half way. It was a perilous nap for him, but one, no doubt, he was accustomed to.

Indians always speak in the masculine, third person singular, when alluding to persons or things, and the phrase "may be so" is constantly introduced into their conversations.

They speak very broken English, and I found they understood me much better when I spoke to them in the same way, a correct and connected speech, seeming to confuse them.

Last night's march fatigued us all very much, so that we slept long and soundly.

The day passed in reading, writing and dozing, with the thermometer at one hundred in the shade, and nightfall found the train *"streched out"* as it is called, and all ready for the road.

The day's repose put us all in order for the enjoyment of our ride, which was a long one, but under such a sky and in such a country time and space are easily annihilated.

We passed at midnight a singular mound upon the open prairie, which we ascended and had an extensive moonlight view.

This mound was evidently natural, curious from the fact, that it was the only mass of earth and rock in sight rising from the surface, and that it rose abruptly, from a narrow base, to a height of over one hundred feet.

It was doubtless the remains of the ancient super strata of prairie, which worn by time and washing, has fallen from the level of the great Llano Exetacao, to its present general surface.

At daylight we encamped upon a tributary of Red River.—

July 9th. Turning night into day does well enough for cattle and horses, but its effect upon the human biped was very perceptible in the lounging step, the hearty yawn and the disordered look of every one and everything about camp.

Our Indians, were the only ones stirring until a late hour, and when we turned out, two deer were ready for the spit, the proceeds of their morning's work.

I have been struck with the thorough going manner of these Delawares.

When anything was to be done, not even conversation was indulged in until it was finished.

So soon as they had deposited their game at the door of the Captain's tent, they turned their attention to drying the skins ; this they did by stretching them in every part by means of long thin sticks, fastened upon the hair side, and then hanging them in the sun, and air. After this—as this was their day to draw rations of sugar, coffee and flour—bread was baked and coffee roasted, they then prepared a meal, and afterwards lounged, chatting, smoking or dozing, until the time for making ready for the road, a good example, worthy of imitation, business first, ease afterwards.

Having observed another mound about, as I thought, a quarter of a mile off, I started on foot to explore it, when, to my surprise, an hour elapsed ere I reached the top, so deceptive are distances on the prairie.

This mound was more elevated, but less abrupt than the former one.

I found on top a rude structure, built of loose stones, but

9*

whether intended as an altar for sacrifice, or constructed as an additional land mark, it was impossible to tell.

Some buffalo bones were strewn around, and I roused a large grey eagle from his eyrie on the rocks; who, evincing rather a hostile manner, I thought most prudent to make my descent; not before, however, enjoying the view, decidedly the finest sunset scene I had yet met with.

There is a kind of grass, which grows on the prairie, in patches, resembles timothy, and when in seed has a long shining cottony head. It required but little stretch of the imagination to form these patches into lakes, glistening in the sunset, so that with our large herd feeding, tents pitched, and white covered wagons, dotting the plain, I had as fine a pastoral scene before me as could be desired.

The bustle in camp and the lengthening shadows admonished me that it was time to mount; so hastening back, Lieut. C——n, the Doctor, and myself, mounted, took the head of the train, and led off on our grass-grown way. Soon an object appears on the distant horizon, "a deer," said one, "a horse," said another," "no, its a man," we all exclaim together. Now the sight of a strange face and form, in those wilds, is by far the most remarkable that can be met with. It is like meeting with a strange sail at sea; curiosity and suspicion are both aroused, so that the moment a human form is descried, every one is on the alert. "Let us reconnoitre," was our first exclamation, after deciding upon the genus in the distance, so away we went, when, lo and behold, our "ould citizen feller" again. Poor old wretch, he had become bewildered, from fatigue, hunger and thirst, and turning round in his tracks, was travelling away from, instead of towards the fort. Humanity now prompted Lieut. C——n to put him in charge of the guard, so that he reached Fort Belknap without any further adventures.

Our march was a very long one, but a party of us managed to get to the camping ground about midnight, where, building a fire, we resigned ourselves to sleep until the train came up.

CHAPTER VIII.

JULY 10th.—Our camp was on the head waters of the
South fork of the Little Witchita.

At this point the stream did not run at this season, but we
found plenty of water in holes in the bed.

Some years since, Captain Marcy (in passing along this
route with a command,) encamped at this point, and notices—
in his report—a singular phenomena, which, to superstitious
minds, would have been taken for a great and good omen.

Arriving here, he found the bed of the stream entirely dry,
but dispatching men up its course to search for water, they
soon came running back, shouting, "look out boys, here
comes plenty of water;" and sure enough the river soon ran
bank full. The Captain supposes that the water had been
dammed up by brush wood, &c., and suddenly burst through
in sufficient quantity to create the apparent miracle. On
such grounds many so called supernatural events may be
explained.

After breakfast, this morning, the Captain started (as was his usual custom when in camp) to hunt and explore in the neighbourhood. He returned with news of having seen tracks of quite a herd of buffalo, a most unusual thing now in this country, and which excited us all very much, as a buffalo hunt is the prime sport of the prairies.

This animal is rapidly disappearing from the plains. But eight years since, herds roamed around the City of Austin, and were frequently seen in the streets; now there are but few to be found south of Red River, so that a sight even, but of all things a chase, would have been an episode in our camp life, affording us both interest and excitement. As the species is becoming extinct, all facts connected with their history become interesting and important.

They were once found in countless herds over almost the whole continent of North America, from Lake Champlain to the Rocky Mountains, and from the twenty-eighth to the fiftieth degree of North latitude, and were then only killed in quantity sufficient to furnish the Indian with food, clothing and lodges, but the havoc made among them by white men for their skins, and thousands of them for their *tongues alone*, has thinned their numbers, and driven them to a narrow section of country, between the settlements and the base of the Rocky Mountains. A few extracts from ancient authors may not be uninteresting in connection with this subject.

In a work published at Amsterdam, in 1637, called "New English Canaan," by Thomas Morton, one of the first settlers of New England, he says, "The Indians have also made description of great *heards* of well *groune* beasts that live about the parts of this lake (Erocoise), now Lake Champlain, such as the Christian world (until this discovery,) hath not *bin* made acquainted with.

"These beasts are of the bigness of a *cowe*, their flesh being very good *foode*, their hides good leather; their fleeces very useful, being a kind of *woole*, as fine almost as the *woole* of the beaver; and the *salvages* do make garments thereof.

"It is *tenne yeares* since first the relation of these things came to the *eares* of the English."

Another author (Purchas) states, that as early as in 1613, the adventurers in Virginia discovered a "slow *kinde* of *cattell* as *bigge* as kine, which were good *meate*."

In a work published in London, in 1589, by Hukluyt, it is stated, that in the island of New Foundland were found "*mightie beastes*, like to camels in greatness, and their *feete* were cloven." He then says, "I did see them *farre* off, not able to *discerne* them perfectly, but their steps showed that their *feete* were cloven, and *bigger* than the *feete* of camels. I suppose them to be a kind of *buffes*, which I read to *bee* in the *countreys* adjacent, and very many in the *firme* land."

Colonel Fremont publishes some interesting statistics of these animals, in his report, and states the number ascertained to have been slaughtered in one year (1849) to be *six hundred thousand*. With this rapid diminution in their numbers, they must in a few years be entirely exterminated.

During the morning, Wagon brought in a doe and fawn. It made me sad to see the delicate little fawn stretched upon the grass, cold and dead. I enjoyed the rich, juicy flesh, 'tis true, but the means taken to procure it went against my feelings.

Our Delawares, used a little instrument called a bleat, to lure the does ; it is made in two pieces, the lower one precisely like the upper part of a *clarionet ;* On this is fitted a hollow mouth piece, and by closing the end of the lower piece, filling the upper with air and opening and shutting the lower alternately, the cry of the fawn is imitated so exactly as to lure the doe within shot, thus making the affection of the mother for her young, the means of her death, a piece of barbarity which I could not sanction, though I must confess my prairie appetite overcame my scruples under the influence of the savoury odour of the smoking haunch.

It is not always consistent with safety to use the bleat in a wild country, as sometimes a panther or a bear may be attracted by the sound, and unless the hunter has his wits about him, he may suffer for his sport.

The following incidents, which happened during a former expedition, will illustrate this. Captain Marcy, endeavoured to lure one of a herd of antelopes, that were feeding some distance from him, one day when away from camp, when just as he was in the act of firing upon one, which had been decoyed within range of his rifle, his attention was drawn to a rustling in the grass, and to his surprise, he saw an enormous panther, bounding towards him and within twenty paces. Instantly changing the direction of his rifle, he fired and succeeded in dispatching the animal—the Indian guide also, once lured a doe and fawn within range, when a panther anticipated him by seizing the fawn, but was immediately shot.

A large horned adder was added to our collection to-day, sunset found us again on the march, and ten miles brought us to a branch of the Trinity where we fixed our camp for the next day.

July 11th.—The country we had been passing over, since leaving the Cross Timbers, was a rolling prairie, very thin in soil and timber very scarce.   At this point we began to find the Mesquite trees in great abundance.

This growth is a very singular one, variously called Mesquite, Mezkeet, Musquit and Muckeet.   The trees grow short and scrubby, seldom attaining a height of twenty feet, with the trunk, from four to fifteen inches in diameter.   The limbs are short, crooked and very thickly studded with sharp thorns.   The leaf is pinnated, long, and the leaflets elliptical, the bark a dark gray, resembling that of the peach tree, the wood coarse grained and very brittle, with the heart like dark mahogany.   It burns readily, with a clear flame, leaving a very hot and perfect coal, like hickory.

The trees grow singly, and at such regular intervals as to resemble a plantation, and so much like a peach orchard that one cannot divest himself of the idea, in entering a grove, that he is approaching a house, and involuntarily listens for the watch-dog's bark, or some other sign of human habitation

So much so is this the case that the sutler at Fort Belknap, relates a laughable incident (connected with this subject) of one of his teamsters, who one evening, on the route from Fort Smith, with a load of stores, got behind the train, and on coming into camp without his team, was asked where he had left it, " Out in that old peach orchard," was his reply.

They bear a long slender bean, from which a cooling beverage is made by the Mexicans, and being saccharine and nutritious, is used for food by the Indians on the plains, and makes excellent forage for horses and mules.

It affords a gum, which exudes from any bruise or incision, and no doubt will answer all the purposes of the gum arabic, in fact it belongs to the same family as the acacia.

The mesquite is almost the only tree to be found over a vast region in the South West, and from its many useful qualities, among which, not the least is its durability for building purposes—will be invaluable to the future settlers.

The distressed condition of our oxen, determined the Captain to precede the train, go in to Fort Belknap—forty miles off—complete his arrangements and meet us fifteen miles out, from which point we commenced our unexplored journey into the wilds of Texas.

We were all soon busy in writing the few last words home which it would be our privilege to send for a long time.

Hearts and homes, sweet words of pleasure, how clings
10

affection round your memories. The sunny hours of childhood, the sterner realities of manhood, the ties of filial and domestic affection, all crowd upon the thoughts at such a moment, never so fully appreciated, so fondly loved, as when about to say farewell perhaps forever. We all felt the influence of our solitude and isolation, and sadly wore the day away until sunset brought the hour of preparation for our midnight march.

During the day three new species of lizards, and several fish were added to our collection. In the afternoon the Captain and the Doctor left us, and marching at nightfall, eight miles brought us again to the Trinity where we encamped.

Shortly after getting to camp, it was determined to kill an ox, who had broken a horn and was quite unruly.

An hour had not elapsed, before we had a beautiful concert of whines, yells and barks from a pack of at least one hundred wolves, who snuffing the blood, stationed themselves around us and kept up their hungry serenade until day dawned.

The wolf met with here, was the gray species, with a long bushy tail, very cowardly and voracious.

Their tone is not a howl, but a whining yell ending in a short quick bark, both mournful, monotonous and grating on the ear, and very effectual in driving away sleep, when surrounded by such a host as annoyed us that night.

July 12th. The prairie around our camp was very much broken, and the soil barren,

A stroll, in search of better grass, brought Lieut C———n and myself to an old Indian camp, where we found some beads and other relics.

We also saw numerous tracks of wild horses, where they had come to drink at a water hole in the prairie, which was at this time dry.

Tarantulas and centipedes abounded in great numbers, and we made quite a collection of very large specimens.

Nightfall, as usual, found us on the march, but on account of the scarcity of water we made slow progress, and finding a good spring on the open prairie, we encamped near it.

July 13th.—The prairie was still much broken and rough, affording a fine field for our collections in natural history, among the rocks and ravines. We took advantage of it, and lizards, rattlesnakes, and the insect tribe, were brought in in numbers.

One of the men brought me a most singular and beautiful vine. It was the wild passion flower, at that season bearing both fruit and flowers. The flower is similar to the one known in the conservatories North, and the fruit is about the size of a nectarine, of a brilliant red colour on the outside and orange inside. It looked very inviting, but is not edible. I collected the seeds, however, intending to try how it will stand our northern climate, where, should it flourish, it will make a most graceful and gorgeous ornament for the arbor or portico.

We marched at sunset, Lieut. P———e going in advance to

find water. He left word that wherever he found it he would build a fire as a signal. Several hours elapsed when we saw a fire some distance off the road. Supposing of course that it was his, Lieut. C——n and myself rode up to it, when we suddenly found ourselves in a hunting camp of Kickapoos.

We had several times remarked upon the scarcity of game on our route, having seen only an occasional deer, and those brought in by the Indians, causing them to hunt long distances from the direct line of march. This scarcity was now explained; the Kickapoos are the most famous hunters known, and when they pass over a section of country game almost disappears for a season.

Their plan is to hunt in sufficient numbers to cover a long line of country, and moving forward in this order, with their families, pack-horses, &c., they sweep off every thing before them. Their women were busy dressing skins and drying venison. The skins were stretched around a square frame, made of poles stuck in the ground, with a fire built in the middle ; the meat they cut in long thin strips and laid it on top of poles bent into a semicircle, forming a kind of large coop, and then built a slow fire underneath.

It was a wild scene, at the murk hour, to come upon these naked dusky savages bustling in the lurid glare of their fires, and looking like so many demons from the background where we stood.

We found tolerable water near them, both in quantity and quality, and concluded to encamp for the night.

After pitching tents we visited them again, when they offered us some venison and seemed quite friendly.

An old and very gaudy dressing-gown which I wore, attracted their particular attention, and one of the squaws attempted to gratify her curiosity by handling me with her great greasy paws, but I kept moving round about and avoided contact, as nothing could be more disgusting than these copper-colored greasy wenches, naked except a filthy rag around their loins, their skins reeking with perspiration, and hair matted and uncombed. We soon gratified our curiosity and returned to camp.

Just as we were about to retire to our blankets, voices were heard in the distance and two young officers from the fort drove up, giving us the intelligence that the Captain and the Doctor were safe, and that eight miles further we should reach the Cottonwood Spring, a well-known camping-ground for troops passing to and fro, and the spot designated by the Captain where we were to await his return with Major Neighbours and the additional Indian hunters and guides.

It was now midnight, but the order was given, and in a short time we were off to the cool water, where we arrived just as day dawned; fatigued, but fortunate in reaching the only really good water we had had since leaving the Basin Spring. A few hours sleep and we were all right again.

CHAPTER IX.

CAMP AT THE COTTON WOOD SPRING.

Officers leave.—Description of Camp.—Wild Indians come in.—Treatment of Squaws.—Visit of the Indians.—Indian Bivouac.—Departure of Indians.— Captain and party arrive.—Major Neighbours.—Description of our Indian Corps.

July 14th.—The young officers returned to the fort this morning, accompanied by Lieutenant P——e, leaving Lieutenant C——n, and myself alone in camp.

We were encamped in a pleasant mesquite grove, in sight of the cool spring, and though the weather was hot, a fine breeze so tempered the atmosphere that our stay was very reviving after night marches, with muddy rain-water to drink.

Whilst lying in our tents, about noon, we descried some objects advancing over the brow of the hill in front of camp, and soon found them to be a party of To-wac-o-nies and Waco's on their return from Fort Belknap.

They halted a short distance from our camp, and the women commenced putting up their temporary shelter, from sun and storm, which they constructed of boughs, skins, blankets, &c.

The chief—(an ugly old creature, a fac simile of a superannuated monkey,) soon rode up, and dismounting near his half finished lodge, threw himself upon the grass, whilst his wife—about to become a mother—stopped her work, immediately, to unbridle, unsaddle and tether his horse, for of course, he disdained the smallest labour or assistance to her.

The principal use the wild Indian makes of his wife or wives is to wait upon him, she takes his horse and attends to it when he halts, saddles, bridles and brings it up when he wishes to ride, cooks his meals, puts up the temporary lodge or shealting, and dresses what skins may be obtained in the chase, in fact, does all the manual labour necessary in their wandering life.

Her lord lounges, sleeps, drinks, smokes, eats, fights, hunts, and not unfrequently, *rewards* her with a sound drubbing, the only extra physical exertion he ever makes.

In the afternoon, the old chief made us a visit. He was full of affection for the whites, and showed us a certificate of character, (no doubt written by some worthless scamp, as we ascertained the old fellow to be a most arrant knave and horse-thief,) from which we learned his name to be Ak-a-quash.

He was very importunate in his begging propensities, and not at all modest in his demands, as the sequel proved.

He wanted meat, tobacco, flour, coffee and sugar, not salt meat either, for that he got at Belknap ; and taking up some yellow sand in his fingers, he said, " Belknap suker so." Meaning that he wanted white sugar ; pretty well for a wild Indian, living the precarious life they do. We told him he must be satisfied with what he could get, not what he wanted, and he did not refuse what we offered him.

Soon after, the whole gang gathered round, and then such a chattering among the squaws, like so many monkeys, running round and handling every thing and begging for every thing they saw.

A son of the old Chief made his appearance last, in full *court costume*, and a most laughable sight he was.

He had on a pair of moccasins, leggings made out of an old pair of soldier's pantaloons, a blue breech cloth, and an old greasy, summer sack coat, over which he wore an old fashioned full uniformed infantry coat *minus one tail*, the other, as Ak-a-quash told us, having been cut off by one of his comrades to get at his bottle of whiskey, whilst he lay drunk and asleep at Fort Belknap. His face was painted half a dozen colours, his ears loaded down with large brass rings, and with a shock head of hair, to one of the side locks of which was attached an old red worsted comforter, he presented the most ludicrous figure imaginable, more particularly as he seemed so well pleased with himself, and strutted about like a young turkey cock.

Among his other accomplishments he had learned to swear, and kept repeating two oaths constantly in all he had to say.

How strange the perversion, that man, whether civilized or savage, is so apt to copy vice, so slow to imitate virtue !

To attempt to teach the savage to read, to write, to sow, to reap, is a thankless undertaking; to learn him to smoke, to drink, to swear, can be effected in the shortest time, and by any tyro in vicious indulgence.

Pretty soon, however, the young dandy had his pride and consequence humbled.

Ak-a-quash was very importunate for something to drink, and as we had no spirits of any kind to give him, we offered him some lemonade, made with citric acid and oil of lemon. He drank it quite greedily, which the youth observing, held out his hand for a glassful; he drank it, but it proved too much for his stomach, irritated by his late debauch; a pipe of tobacco and the acid together, to use a common saying, *fixed him*, the consequences I leave to imagination, suffice it to say he left as soon as he could get the use of his legs.

By this time they had become very annoying to us, the day was oppressively hot, and the squaws keeping up such a chattering and running around, and the necessity of watching them closely to prevent them stealing, so that ordering up the commissary corporal, some beef, flour and sugar were handed to them, and pointing to the hill-top, we told them as plainly as signs could, to be off, which they did, not before, however, making another attack upon our sugar bowl and tobacco box.

I obtained a great curiosity from one of the sub chiefs in this party. It was a pair of ear-rings made out of a species of sea shell variegated and brilliant. They are said to be brought from the islands of the Pacific Coast, and to find their way to these wanderers through the traders. They were very large and massive.

The sub chief was badly shod, having on an old pair of torn prunella gaiter boots. He took a fancy to a pair of stout walking shoes I had, but chaffered a good while before bargaining. He was willing to give one for both, but I said by signs, one ear-ring, one shoe; he took it, supposing perhaps that I would give him the other, but after waiting awhile he pointed to the other shoe and held out his other ear-ring, when I gave him the shoe, took the ear-ring, and he went off satisfied.

These Indians go entirely naked, except the breech cloth, unless chance or crime throws some garment into their way, and laughable enough they look sometimes, as for instance— One of the squaws had not an article of clothing on her but an old filthy rag round her loins, and *a gay calico sun bonnet on her head.*

The squaws were tattoed on the breast and face; in lines on the face, and circles on the breasts.

Their young children—of which there were six or eight with the party—were entirely naked—not wearing the breech cloth —but seemed healthy, and were amusing themselves with miniature bows and arrows.

In the evening, Lieutenant C———n and myself visited their bivouac, when they all came out "in puris naturalibus," and danced to the devil's tattoo, beat upon the bottom of a tin can by one of the men, a wild, monotonous chaunt being kept up at the same time by the dancers, varied by short yells and grunts, upon the whole a very disgusting scene, as young " *sans*" *coat tail* swore a great deal, and took liberties with the squaws not very agreeable to eyes polite.

One old squaw, with a head of long, matted white hair, pointed first to the stalwart men among the dancers and then to her naked, shrivelled breasts, thereby informing us that five of them were her sons, and then pointing to one of the squaws and a boy along side, showed by signs that he was her grandson. She also, by raising her hands seven times, with her fingers spread open, informed us she was seventy years old.

We soon left, quite satisfied that were we to take them prisoners and either confine or kill them, in either case we would be doing good service, for except their greater capacity for mischief, there was no difference between them and the wolves, which at the time, were keeping their nightly patrol around camp in search of plunder.

July 15th.—The Indians left this morning, passing by our camp in true Indian style, viz., Ak-a-quash first, carrying nothing but his weapons, then the men of the party, and last, the squaws, some with a child tied in a bag and fastened around her loins, or seated upon a bundle of skins, upon the horse's croup.

The women rode astride, and their duty was to drive the pack horses and take care of the baggage, this being done even by the aged squaw, naked and bareheaded, but astride upon a pack, and armed with a whip, labouring away at the straggling pack horses, whilst her great louts of sons and grandsons rode along, listless, naked, and brutal, thinking of nothing but where they should get their next meal, or steal their next lot of horses; truly, thought I, what is the use in spending time and money at this age of the world, to encourage such brutality and vice.

In the evening the Captain, Doctor, and Major Neighbours arrived. They brought with them three Delawares and a Shawnee, the addition to our Indian force which we expected, thus making our corps of guides and hunters six strong.

Major Neighbours was a fine looking man, in the full vigour of manhood, about six feet two inches in height, with a countenance indicative of great firmness and decision of character.

He was the Indian Agent for Texas, and joined the expedition to assist in the explorations and locations, a service which his great experience and judgment peculiarly fitted him for.

The Delawares and Shawnees fraternizing so well, are often employed together on such expeditions.

The new-comers were well known to our two quondam hunters, and observing that they all had the same Christian name, and called each other brother, I was curious to ascertain how so many brothers could have the same name. Upon inquiry I found they were children of sisters, consequently cousins. We now had John Connor, John Jacobs, John Wagon, John Jackson, John Jacobs, jun., and John Hunter, the Shawnee.

John Connor was the leader and interpreter. He was a fine, portly man, about forty-five years old, and very light complexioned, with long black hair and moustache, more like an Arab than an Indian.

The costume of this party consisted of hunting-shirt, leggins, breech cloth and moccasins; their accoutrements simple and entirely for service. They carried flint-locked rifles, with a knife, powder-horn and ball-pouch, an awl, charger, and a whetstone in a case, all slung to a broad belt, and ready to put on at a moment's warning. In addition they carried pistols, as one of them observed, " May be so now we got two shoots, any how."

The Shawnee was a noble specimen of his race. His complexion was a dark, reddish copper; his figure short, athletic, and all bone and muscle. He wore a black moustache, and disdaining any head gear, with a bushy growth of black hair, looked the very embodiment of wild vigor and endurance, either for the fight or the chase.

We found him to be a splendid hunter, bold rider, and, though only twenty-two years old, a very reliable guide.

We felt all the safer for this addition to our forces, and commenced our doubtful and dangerous journey under most favorable auspices, our men being all in fine health.

11

CHAPTER X.

COTTONWOOD SPRING TO DIVIDING RIDGE.

Leave the road.—Description of country from Red River.—Stock raising in Texas.—Buck killed.—Indian cookery.—Description of Bluffs.—Kickapoo grave.—Cactus seen.—Deer called up by bleat.—Mesquite Beans.—Bridging Ravines.—Black Flies.—Cross Crater.—Snakes shot.—Arrive at Little Witchita.—Mesquite Grass.—Indian signs.—Manner of lariating.—Valley of Witchita.—Fine scenery on the Plains.—Antelope killed.—Anxiety about Horses.—Jackass Rabbit killed.—Breezes on the Plains.—Exploring Party leave.—Arrive at branch of Big Witchita.—Repairing Wagons.—Intense weather.—Effect of the atmosphere.—Oxen missing.—Reach the Little Witchita.—Exploring Party return.—Insects on the Plains.—Fawn chase.—Camanche graves.—Reach the Divide.

JULY 16th.—So far we had had the advantage of the military road from Fort Washita to assist us with our heavy train. We had now to leave this and striking into the vast plains which compose unexplored Texas, to travel entirely by compass, make our own roads, and trust to the state of the case for water, grass, and whatever else might be necessary to accomplish the objects of our expedition.

From Red River to this point, nothing can surpass the facilities of the country for stock-raising, sufficient to mark Texas as the great stock-yard of our country in the future.

The same advantages prevail here that exist in those countries where stock-raising is followed as a business, and will attain the same results.

Water is plenty, the whole country being intersected with creeks and rivers, and although the season was unprecedently dry, we met with no scarcity even on our narrow line of march.

The grass remains green and nutritious throughout the winter-months, and there is plenty of timber for building or firewood for the herdsman.

There are in Texas between one and two millions of horned cattle, and the same management prevails throughout the State. The plan is to sell out all the beeves from four years old and upwards. The cows are never sold or killed for beef, but kept expressly for breeding. The increase in stock cattle is twenty-five per cent. annually, and in some instances more. This compounded yearly will produce in a series of years immense results. This increase is certain, for cattle seldom die except from old age. The territory is large enough to cut five states as large as New York out of it, and with such economy in management and such ·facilities of range, who can realize what immense herds will eventually roam all over these prairies, or the immense income Texas will receive from this source alone.

After breaking up camp, we gradually ascended in a north-west course, over a rolling country, covered with buffalo grass and mesquite timber, stopping every few miles to admire the fine panorama stretched out before us, vast and picturesque as it was, and enjoying the delicious breeze, which though the thermometer stood at one hundred in the shade was exhilarating and refreshing, our party all in fine spirits and full of enthusiasm for the new scenes we were to pass through.

After an hour or two's march, one of our party saw a blanket tied to a mesquite tree, and fluttering in the distance. Such signals are always to be approached with caution on the plains, as they are almost invariably a decoy of some lurking savage, who thus, by exciting curiosity, lures his victim within range of the deadly rifle or arrow.

Approaching it cautiously, our guide, John Conner, gave us the agreeable intelligence, that John Jacobs, who had been sent in advance to seek for water and camping ground, had shot a fat buck and took this means of calling our attention to it; and a noble specimen he was, very fat, with a full head of horns just in the velvet,* so that instead of a Caman-che, we had caught a gem for the larder. He was soon skinned and ready for transportation to camp.

We marched on, with the rays of a glorious sunset pro-longing the evening until a late hour shining upon us, and

* Bucks first have horns when three years old.—The horns are then short and unbranching.

They shed them every year, and each succeeding head of horns has an addi-tional branch.

Whilst the horns are growing to full size, they are covered with a soft velvety skin. This is what is meant by *horns in the velvet.*

The horns now begin to itch and make the animal restless, who to relieve himself rubs them in the bushes and against the trees until the velvet disap-pears, and the solid bone is discovered underneath. At the time of rubbing off the velvet, the bucks have a singular appearance, the whole head and neck being covered with blood and the velvety skin hanging in shreds from the horns.

encamped upon so fine a stream that in anticipation of future wants the Captain ordered our water-barrels to be filled.

The Major, an old campaigner, whose mouth had been watering for a taste of the juicy buck, immediately gave orders to one of the Indian corps, and soon the smoking ribs invited us to a feast which needed no Appician appetite to enjoy.

The way in which Indians cook venison is peculiar. Sharpening a stick at both ends, the meat is spitted upon it, the stick stuck in the ground near a blazing fire and the meat watched closely, turning it occasionally until the gravy begins to run, when with the simple addition of salt a morsel is prepared which once tasted leaves a lasting impression upon the palate, light and easy of digestion, and carrying no nightmare with it. We enjoyed it fully, and slept soundly under the effects.

July 17th.—We marched at sunrise, our course still northwest. In a short time the scene changed, and we were amidst the first bold scenery we had yet encountered. Long ranges of precipitous bluffs bounded the horizon, looking like so many barriers to our future progress. These bluffs were of igneous formation, and afforded a fine field for the geologist.

In many places large slabs of sandstone were poised upon pencils of red clay, looking like a miniature Stone Henge, or the ruins of the Pantheon, the whole presenting a singular feature in the landscape.

11*

We found some curious specimens of the cactus—perfectly round and flat, not more than three or four inches thick, but many of them five feet in diameter.

We also passed a Kickapoo grave, which our guide pointed out to us, and described their manner of burial. He said, " He dig him hole deep like man, den stick him in head up, and may be so he leave him,"—a singular mode of burial, truly.

A doe and buck were called up on the open prairie by means of the bleat, showing how effectual this little instrument is in expert hands. One of our amateurs tried a shot at them, but failed to hit, and they bounded off over the plain and were soon lost to sight.

We crossed the west fork of the Trinity, and after nooning proceeded to make a bridge of gum elastic timber over a ravine that ran across our course. This tree is not the *caoutchouc*, but takes its name from the berry, which is edible, and like the prepared gum elastic of commerce, is springy.

The mesquite trees here began to show the beans, which are similar—though narrower—to the honey locust, and being full of saccharine matter, our Indians seemed very fond of them, pulling and eating them by handfuls as they rode along.

The wild passion-flower also abounded here in great profusion, festooning the trees and looking very tempting, relieved by the deep green foliage. I collected a good store of the seeds.

After crossing the ravine, we passed through a succession

of low hills, giving us, at every few moments, beautiful changes of scenery, and at sunset encamped upon a small fork of the Trinity.

To-day, our oxen suffered terribly from the attacks of large black flies, which came in myriads.

They were as large as humble bees, and very voracious; their proboscentes inflicting wounds deep enough to keep the blood flowing after the insects fell off from repletion.

We felt very anxious about our stock, as these flies, with scarcity of water, which we expected to encounter, would tell most fearfully upon them, but hoped, as we rose higher, to get rid of them.

July 18th.—Our course to-day was West, towards the head waters of the Little Witchita, passing through fine ranges of bluffs, affording many fine views, but the country so broken that the working party were constantly employed bridging creeks, ravines and branches.

We passed through the crater of an old volcano, which must have been in activity before the flood, from surrounding indications, the ground being covered with scoriæ, among which were found fossils.

The Major shot a prairie snake, a species of adder, about eleven feet long, and a rattlesnake, a most formidable reptile, full seven feet long, with teeth an eighth of an inch in length, and eleven rattles. Both these specimens were prepared for our collection.

Happening to remark that I thought it fortunate rattlesnakes were so seldom met with, Conner replied, "may be so, in de timber and valley, dere you catch him great many, out here in de prairie, fire burn all up."

Every one that we met with was sure to be despatched, and though the dimensions given appear fabulous, yet I can vouch for their accuracy, for their size so astonished me, that I was minute enough to measure each one described with a tape line.

We nooned under a live oak, the first specimen we had met with. All the timber thus far, from the Belknap road, having been gum elastic, mesquite, and a few cotton wood trees near the streams.

In the afternoon we marched only one mile, and reaching a branch of the Little Witchita, found that so much work was to be done, bridging the stream and digging down the banks, that we could not expect to cross before sundown, which we did, and encamped in an old Kickapoo camp, on a plain covered with mesquite grass. I employed the evening in gathering the seed, now fully ripe, with the intention of introducing it into the Northern States. This grass, having a long head upon it like oats, yields two crops during the year, is very hardy and good alike either for pasture or fodder; the cultivation of it among the farmers in Texas who have tried it, has proved very flattering and productive.

At this camp—plenty of Indian signs being visible—much additional precaution was taken, horse stealing being a universal propensity with the savage. Their plan is to crawl into camp, unlariat a horse, and springing upon his back start off at full speed, thus making a stampede among the others, which is generally successful.

The government tried the experiment—some years since—of hobbling the dragoon horses—when on the plains—with iron hobbles, but had to abandon it, as the Indians invariably killed the horse when they could not get him off.

Our horses during the trip were all secured by rope lariats thirty feet long, fastened round their necks with an iron picket pin, about eighteen inches long, at one end, to be driven into the ground.

The Delawares secured their horses by fastening a short loop of raw hide around both fore legs, below the knees, so that the horse could only move slowly and by a succession of jumps, something like a kangaroo. Another plan is to fasten the long lariat around the fetlock, but the greatest precaution fails to secure stock inevitably from the wily savage, as sometimes a party will dress in skins, having bundles of deer's hoofs attached, and carrying rattles made of the hoofs in their hands, then near morning when all is quiet they sweep through camp with loud yells and rattling of the hoops, and creating a panic amongst the animals are generally successful to some extent; often, however, sweeping off the whole herd.

July 19th.—Moving to-day in a north-west course, we had a fine view of the valley of the Witchita.

Towering in the background were the long battlemented

bluffs lining the opposite shore of the river below, the green belt of timber marking its course, and in front the wide prairie with its yellow coating of buffalo grass, studded with the pale green mesquite, a beautiful combination for a landscape painting.

My wonder has been throughout my journey that so few if any of our artists ever join expeditions to the plains. A portfolio could soon be filled with novelties, compared with which the hackneyed subjects universally to be found on sale or exhibition sink into mediocrity. Every variety can be found there, hill, dale, lake, valley, mountain, river and plain, whilst color, tint, light and shade are constant in quantity and quality. Let but the experiment be tried, and prairie scenery will become a valued gem in the gallery.

Why is it that no one returns from the plains disappointed. It is because their anticipations have been doubly realized. This fact is to my mind conclusive, that visits of artists to the plains would not only end in adorning the art, but give a better impression of that comparatively "terra incognita." I say a better, not a full impression, for to be fully realized it must be seen and passed over.

We nooned near another crater, which, like the former, was very ancient; the ground being covered with scoriæ, worn and abraded by time and weather. We found a new species of cactus, growing like a tree, the stalk and branches having a woody fibre, and studded with the thorny pulp peculiar to that plant.

The largest rattlesnake yet killed was added, by the Major's unerring six shooter, to our collection—eight feet long and eleven rattles. Wagon shot a buck antelope, the first we had had in camp. They resemble the goat more than the deer, and the flesh also tastes more like goat's flesh.

This specimen—a full grown buck—had a full head of horns, short, of a shining black color, with one branch. His head was an ornament to our collection.

The antelope is the fleetest animal known on the plains, greyhounds, which Captain Marcy had with him on a former expedition, never having been able to overtake one, though they ran down many of the red deer and jackass rabbits. He says that the longer the chase continued between the antelope and the hounds, the greater the distance seemed to be between them.

The soil was red clay and very poor, in fact all the soil thus far from the Belknap road, was, with little exception, very thin.

On the afternoon's march one of the party killed a jackass rabbit, a very large species, called jackass, from the length of its ears. It resembles the English hare in color and general appearance. This specimen had ears nine inches long and standing perfectly erect upon its head ; its body from tip to tip was seventeen inches long, and height ten inches. It made a very savoury breakfast dish.

We reached the main Witchita for our evening camp, and after a bath in the brackish water of the stream, made a sumptuous repast off the ribs of the antelope, cooked by the inimitable John Hunter, the Shawnee, the very pink of perfection in the art of Indian cookery.

July 20th.—Our Indian scouts having reported the country beyond our camp, in the direction we were traveling, inaccessible to our heavy train, the Captain determined to rest during the day, whilst preparations were made to explore further with a small party mounted and accompanied by pack mules.

We now found how judicious was the filling of our water-barrels. The water in the river was undrinkable by man, being salt and bitter. Our animals drank it, but with no good results, only as a necessity. It gave them cramps, made them restless and emaciated, and in the end would have proved fatal.

We had plenty of water in our barrels and were quite comfortable, though the day was oppressively hot; thermometer over one hundred in the shade; but thanks to the delicious breeze of the plains, we suffered but little. This is a striking and very agreeable feature in a prairie tour; the morning opens close and sultry until about nine o'clock, when a breeze springs up, which, not altering the height of the thermometer, renders a grade of one hundred in the shade, or higher, not only tolerable but pleasant. This continues throughout the day, and the nights are cool enough for a blanket.

We were now, by barometer, fifteen hundred feet above the level of the ocean.

Our horses had lately become a source of great anxiety to us. Accustomed to be cornfed and stabled, they had fallen off terribly since fed entirely on grass and picketed in the open air, but this was not all; no horse should ever, on a trip of the kind, be ridden out of a walk, and then only in extreme cases; he should be allowed the freedom of his head, never fretted and never ridden more than fifteen miles in a day, or twenty at the farthest.

Now no man could be more careful of his stock than Captain Marcy, but with all his watchfulness and daily caution, it was impossible to control the wilfulness of some and the inadvertence of others; the results began to show themselves, much to our dissatisfaction. The best kind of stock for such service is mules and Indian ponies; they are raised in the country and acclimated, and this fact was clearly proved on our trip, for whilst those we had were fat and in good spirits, our northern horses were all drooping and miserably thin. As for oxen, I would not take them at all, or if I did, always the Texas cattle. The objections I make to them are these : they suffer from heat, from flies, and the want of water is to them destruction ; besides, they are so miserably slow. I should take mules for draught or packing, and ponies for the saddle. I know that objection is made to horses and mules on account of the depredations of the wild Indians, and the consequent necessity of having a large force

12

of men to guard them at night, but it does seem to me that the anxiety felt when horned cattle are employed, is paramount to the objection ; besides, a trip could be made in less time and with far greater comfort and less loss.

This being the birth-day of one of the young officers, a ration of grog was issued to the men.

The addition to our collection during the day was a large snake, perfectly black, with red lines in diamond on the back. The Indians called it a chicken snake ; the head showed it to be a species of black snake. It had a full-grown rabbit in its maw when opened.

A slight sprinkle of rain—the first for six weeks—followed by a brilliant sunset, closed the day.

July 21st.—The Captain, Major, Doctor, and Lieut. P——e, with a party of four, including two Indians—an essential in all expeditions in this country—left us at an early hour, on their exploring tour, leaving Lieut. C——n and myself alone in camp.

We were sorry to lose the Major, even for a short season ; since he joined our mess, we had received much valuable information and entertainment from his vivid and thrilling descriptions of frontier life in Texas, since its first settlement, with which he was identified.

A plain, practical man, of sound judgment, great energy and common sense, he spoke "to the manor born," no hearsay, but all of which he saw, and part of which he was. An intercourse of fourteen years with the wild Indian tribes, gave him a fund of information and insight into their habits, wants, and the best means of treating with them—invaluable to him in his official capacity, and deeply interesting to the ethnologist and tourist.

The Major had been a state prisoner twenty-two months in the Castle of Perote, during the Texas revolution, and was a fine specimen of a frontier man in the prime of life. His co-operation effected the best results for the expedition.

The Captain having left directions that we should move on slowly in the direction of the Little Witchita, and there wait his return with the exploring party, we moved the train, at eight, A. M., ten miles, to good water, on a branch of the Big Witchita.

Our course had been northerly, passing over a most sterile waste, with the rocks of igneous formation, many of the bluffs stratified with soapstone and abounding in fossil.

One of the Indians shot a spotted jackass rabbit, a very curious specimen, spotted similarly to those kept by the fanciers, evidently not of pure breed, but a cross between the common wild rabbit and this species.*

The day was intensely hot, thermometer one hundred and two degrees in the shade; but arrived at camp, we found a

* I have been met with an objection in describing this specimen, as to its origin, but I can find no evidence that species of the same genus will not propagate in contact with other species of the same genus. On the contrary, the horse and the ass are species of the same genus, and their offspring, the mule; whilst in the case of fowls it is evidenced constantly, the common duck and Muscovy producing an excellent cross for the table; and instances are known of propagation between the dog and the wolf.

deep running stream, filled with catfish, gar and soft turtles. We also found a number of large specimens of the pearl muscle, a beautiful and singular bivalve, which, I have no doubt, would make an excellent substitute for the costly mother of pearl.

During the day, we were recalled to home and civilization, by passing through at least an acre of wild rye, looking just ready for the sickle, an incident which could not fail to make its impression upon us in this remote spot.

With a pleasant bath, and a hearty supper of catfish and coffee, we relished our evening in camp more than ever, our anxiety about water, being removed for the present, which with our thirsty family was no small relief.

July 22d.—I spoke of the stream upon which we were now encamped, as a *running stream*, and to explain. What is called river, creek, or rivulet, in this country, and at this season, refers to the course of the stream, not one in fifty having any water in it, except where the rain-water accumulates in holes in the bed, or some tiny spring trickles out from the bank, no wonder then at the anxiety of the traveller. In the rainy season, the contrary, from the water marks, must be the case, and doubtless then the country is impassable, as it is intersected by dry beds of streams in every direction.

We had enough, and to spare, at this camp, and so halted for the day, until our wagons could be re-tired and prepared for future work. The effect of the atmosphere upon wood of all descriptions, even the best seasoned, was very surprising, causing it to shrink and dry up until nails drew out and bands loosened, requiring constant watching.

The only way, in default of a travelling forge to cut and weld the tires, was to take them off and nail round the wooden rims of the wheels thin laths of pecan, which is best for the purpose, and then heating the tires, draw them on again. As this had to be done to almost every wheel on our wagons, we were fortunate in our camp, as all hands worked cheerfully now that water was plenty.

The atmosphere had the same drying effect upon the skin, and one, who perspired freely, found his face—on cooling in the wind—covered with a fine powder.

There was no dew, and so bland were the nights, that I preferred sleeping in the open air, which I observed the men did, only using the tents as a protection against the heat of the sun, which on this date was awful, thermometer at ten A. M. one hundred and two degrees in the shade ; we were of course better off lying still, under such circumstances, so we amused ourselves with reading, writing and dozing until the moonlight hours for sleep.

Some of the soldiers amused themselves shooting and fishing, but with indifferent success. One said the sun was so hot that the fish would not bite, another that the turkeys were too wild to get a shot at them, all having every reason but the right one, viz., their inexperience and want of skill.

John Jacobs, Jr., Indian-like, saddled his horse and went
12*

off by himself. Not long after, to the surprise and mortification of the amateurs, he returned with a deer across his horse, two turkeys at his saddle-bow, a string of fish in his hand, and two soft turtles. "Ah," said one worthy, "he's up to it, he knows the places;" perhaps he had never been nearer than five hundred miles to this place in his life, but habit was his guide and secret of success.

July 23d.—Early dawn found us all ready to start, but after striking tents and loading wagons, a number of our spare oxen were found to be missing, and as we felt that no doubt we should want them all, in the future, orders were given to unpack and spend the day, which was done with no reluctance, the weather promising to be so intensely hot, and as it proved, thermometer as yesterday at ten A. M., one hundred and two degrees in the shade. Two of the Indians were sent off in search of the oxen. Nothing of interest occurred except that Jacobs discovered a large flock of turkeys on the hill side, and singling out a prime gobbler he pursued it untiringly until he ran it down into camp and there shot it with his pistol, a truly Indian mode of amusement on a hot day.

With the usual routine of camp the day passed quietly, sunset was very gorgeous, and many meteors were seen in the evening, principally from the north-west. Lieutenant C——n and myself made ourselves as happy as circumstances would admit, enduring the heat, and sure of a pleasant night.

July 24th.—Our indefatigable aborigines having brought in

the stray oxen, an early hour found us steering North, over a much better country, and at eleven A. M., we encamped upon a tributary to the Little Witchita, where we found good water and plenty of grass.

As the exploring party had fixed no day for their return to camp, we expected to be detained here some time, but in about an hour after our arrival they came into camp, all very much overcome with heat, thirst and the bad water of the Big Witchita, which they explored some miles towards its mouth, finding a very barren and uninteresting country, with neither grass nor water. They made themselves doubly welcome to us, as they brought in a supply of honey, which they obtained by cutting down a bee tree. They also brought some grey grouse, and the Doctor had found a new and beautiful species of lily, of a brilliant purple, the petal black and cone-shaped. As the Major had never met with it before, we called it the *Camanche Lily.*

Specimens of the soap plant were also found and the seed obtained. This plant grows like the palm, and the Mexicans use the roots for manufacturing a very fine soap. We had a fair opportunity of testing the worth of this soap, as the Major had brought a supply with him from home when he joined our camp. It has a very soothing effect upon the skin when suffering from the attacks of insects, or irritation from sunburn, &c. For ordinary purposes it is as good as the best.

They were all much dissatisfied and prophesied great

suffering in store for us from the want of water, not a very pleasant reflection for us under such an intense sun—thermometer one hundred and four degrees in the shade. The night passed restlessly on account of the attacks of those *humbugs* the mosquitoes.

Gnats, flies, mosquitoes, &c., are all very troublesome on the plains, but all these together cannot compare to the attacks of the most diminutive of the whole insect family, *the red bug.* This little atom—for it is so small that unless upon a shining white surface one cannot see it—is of a brilliant scarlet, and buries itself in the skin in such numbers that the whole surface becomes the color of the insect, causing irritation to such a degree that the contact of clothing is almost unsupportable.

The only relief is to bathe in a strong solution of salt and water, which destroys the insect and allays inflammation, although the remedy is—for a time—almost as bad as the disease.

July 25th.—The morning opened sultry, and sunrise found us on a course West of North, and entering a most desolate region. We were all drooping, when about nine A. M., Jacobs, who was some distance ahead, suddenly turned in his saddles and discharging his rifle at a beautiful fawn, gave a whoop and started in pursuit.

The little creature, frightened, came bounding directly along our line, running the gauntlet of our fire, and half of those mounted started after it, so sympathetic is an incident of this kind, but a jaded horse and a hot day, are poor assistants in a chase, so it ended as it began, in smoke.

A rabbit chase—more successful—shortly afterwards, gave a little more spirit to our party, but our apprehensions about water, soon absorbed every other thought. Oxen cannot get along without it, and it took no small supply for our stock.

We toiled on until noon, under that boiling sun, with the thermometer one hundred and ten degrees *in the shade—the climax of heat during our trip*—and arriving at the foot of a steep bluff, found some rainwater in a hole filled with snakes and green scum, but concluded best to encamp and await the return of Jacobs, who was dispatched ahead to seek for water.

Ascending the bluffs, to get a better view of water courses, &c., we found two Camanche graves. They always bury on the highest peak in their vicinity at the time of the death. The grave is simply a hole scratched in the ground, large enough for the body, and stones piled on top, whether to mark it or as a protection against wolves I know not. I was curious to open one of these graves, and had commenced operations upon it, when Conner came up and with mingled awe and fear in his countenance, remarked "May be so, dis people dey not like dat," so I desisted. I afterwards ascertained, that they bury a corpse in a sitting posture, with clothing, &c., just as it was at the time of death.

From the top of the bluff Conner said he could see the course of the Brazos about forty miles off, and gave us some encouragement, (as many green spots and lines could be seen, marking holes or courses,) that relief was at hand in the shape of water, so that our camp wore a more cheering aspect, though I observed the men made such frequent visits to the water-barrels that a guard had to be placed over them, their minds dwelling so constantly upon thirst as no doubt to increase it, which is invariably the case, not only with this but everything else upon which the mind dwells too long.

Jacobs came in and reported water ten miles off, so that we spent a more comfortable night, for besides, strange to say, the thermometer fell *fifteen degrees* before sundown, and the sky was full of meteors during the evening, principally from the East.

July 26th.—Jacobs was wrong in his estimate of the distance to water; a not unusual thing, as I have before observed, with Indians. Whether this arises from their habit of going to any designated place in the shortest time and by the shortest road or not I know not, but they are seldom accurate in distances ; as for places, they never fail if they have once been there.

We found some tolerable water about four miles from camp, and after watering our stock and taking a supply in our barrels, we continued our march and soon reached the Divide, between the Big Witchita and the Brazos.

This is a high narrow ridge of land, very barren and entirely without water. Water is found on either side, but in spite of the most earnest search none could be found until late in the afternoon, when the Major, always active and on the alert, who had been scouring the country around, found tolerable water both in quantity and quality in a ravine at the foot of a rough and sterile declivity, more than half a mile from any good camping ground.

All this time we had been toiling along the top of the ridge, but now heat and thirst had done its work with our oxen; some laid down in the yoke, some were turned out, and all were panting and lolling their tongues out—a sure sign of exhaustion.

Orders were given to halt and encamp, which we did on the top of the ridge, where there was plenty of buffalo grass, and soon our thirsty animals were refreshed, as far as the limited supply of water would allow, and we making ourselves as comfortable as canvass coverings, with the thermometer at one hundred and six degrees in the shade could make us— the changes in the temperature from heat to cold, and then to heat again, in the last thirty-six hours, being very surprising and trying.

Our course had been west of north, and the Brazos could be seen in the distance about twelve miles from camp.*

---

* It may surprise the reader, that although we had been for some days so near the Little Witchita, the Big Witchita, and the Brazos, three large streams, we should suffer so much for water. The fact is, as the sequel will prove, that these streams take their rise in a gypsum formation, and are so impregnated with this mineral as to be undrinkable. Branches of them contain good water but the main streams are salt and bitter.

We disturbed a herd of antelopes near the water-pool, and several hungry wolves were prowling around in their tracks.

The Captain caught a most curious spider, with the body as large as a pigeon's egg, barred with alternate brown and canary coloured stripes, head brown and armed with a horn, and legs long and black, a new species, and quite an addition to our collection.

This region abounds in iron and copper, and indications are very strong of coal.

CHAPTER XI.

DIVIDING RIDGE TO THE HEAD OF THE BRAZOS.

Water scarce.—Iron and Copper found.—Black Lizard.—Scorpion caught.—Camanche signal.—Preparations for exploring party with pack mules, &c.—
Party leave.—Antelopes seen.—Barren country.—Bad water.—Filling water-
sacks.—Witchita trail.—Conner's sagacity.—Chapparal cock.—Reach Big Witchita.—Quick sands.—Accidents frequent.—Dexterity of Indians in skinning
deer.—Bluffs met with.—Bivouac on bluff.—Fire in bivouac.—Twilight described.—Rattlesnake killed.—Gypsum found.—Stream crooked.—Bitter water·
—Sickness in the party.—Large grasshopper found.—Insects scarce.—Head of
Big Witchita.—Travelling South.—Limestone water found.—Camanche grave.
—Singular ridge.—Man lost.—Bivouac on Brazos.—Alarm in bivouac.—Prairie
Dog town.—Catfish Creek.—Camanche trail.—Rough country.—Singular
knobs.—Hard times.—Man very ill.—Gypsum mountain.—Cross fork of Brazos.—Better country.—Prairie Dogs.—Table Mountain.—Arrive on Llano Estacado.—Head of the Brazos.

JULY 27th.—The Captain being fearful of moving any
farther, in uncertainty about water, despatched Jacobs again
in search, and we remained quietly in camp all day.

The Major and the Doctor explored the country in search
of iron and copper, and came back loaded with specimens,
some very choice.

Whilst writing in my tent, I felt a strange sensation in my
leg and foot, and found that a large black lizard had paid me
a visit. Whether he was anxious to sacrifice his life in the
cause of science or not, I know not, but he paid for his
temerity by a bath in alcohol.

13

The first specimen of the scorpion we have yet met with, was to-day added to our collection, and another fine specimen of the jackass rabbit.

During the day a large column of smoke was seen in the direction of the Brazos, and Conner pronounced it to be made by the Camanches, as a signal, Major Neighbours having sent out runners, before he left home, to tell them that we would be with them about this time, and we had been daily expecting to meet one of the bands.

Jacobs returned and reported having scoured the country for forty miles round and found it dry, barren and broken, but at six miles distance, in a southerly direction, he found good camping ground and tolerable water.

Upon consultation, the Captain determined to move the train to this spot, and leaving it there, to complete the exploration of the head waters of the Big Witchita and Brazos, with pack mules and a small mounted escort.

Report was brought in that sixteen of the oxen were missing, whether having wandered off in search of water and grass, or stolen by the Indians of course could not be told, Jackson and Wagon were despatched in search of them.

July 28th.—Early this morning Conner replied to the Camanche signal, by building a fire upon the top of the highest hill he could find in our vicinity, which was about two miles from camp, when a column of smoke rose high enough to be seen at a distance of forty miles.

The rest of the day was spent in preparations for the exploring party, and in the evening the Indians brought in the stray oxen.

Owing to the bad condition of our horses, we were unable to mount but four men, which with the Captain, Major, Doctor, myself and five Indians, made but a party of thirteen, a small number truly, to attempt the thorough exploration of a country entirely unknown to white men, except as the retiring spot of numerous predatory bands of Indians, after their constant forays upon the frontier settlements; but we had to make the best of what we had, and trust to chance for success.

July 29th.—Leaving the train in charge of the two sub-alterns, our party of thirteen, with nine pack mules and led horses started at day break this morning.

Our course was North-west, and ascending gradually, we came upon a very extensive plain, covered with buffalo grass and mesquite timber. At a short distance south was the dry bed of a lake, covered with luxuriant green grass, and making quite an oasis in the comparative desert around us. Upon this fed the largest herd of antelope we had yet met with. I counted more than thirty in one spot, and deer were plenty.

We rode six miles,* when suddenly and abruptly the scene changed, and a most singular country was brought to view. Below, stretching as far as the eye could reach, was a barren

* We counted distances on our march by the time it took us, and the speed of our horses. With the train we had an odometer, a very curious instrument, fastened in a leather case to the wheels of the ambulance, by which every revolution was counted, and thus the road accurately measured.

and desolate waste, broken and torn into ravines, mounds, gullies and defiles, the soil a bright red clay, and not a tree or a shrub, except the white dwarf cedar, to be seen. Crossing this was like descending the Alps; we had to lead or drive our horses, go single file, and hang on in many places to the cedars that grew in our path.

At the bottom, we found the bed of a large stream, a tributary to the Big Witchita, quite dry, with only a pool of water here and there, standing under the banks, salt and bitter.

This being a foretaste of what we were to expect, the ever vigilant Captain began to think of the future, and cast about for some place to fill our gum-elastic water-bags.

After much search, he found a tiny thread of water trickling down the hill side, and despatched one of the men to dig out a basin to catch it in.

In this way, in an hour's time, we filled our water bags, and drank freely ourselves, when continuing our march over the same barren tract, we nooned near the dry bed of a large creek, where in a hole was brackish water sufficient for our thirsty animals.

In passing down the bed of this stream, in the afternoon, we came upon an Indian trail, when Conner displayed the extraordinary powers he possessed of designating by the mere tracks in the sand the character of the trail.

Riding along with his eyes bent upon the sand, he soon stopped, and said " Witchita trail, may be so, eight animal, two horse, one pony, three mule, horse shod all round, pony too ; shoes on pony old ; one mule shod all round, others shod before ; trail five days old."

How he could be so accurate, he knows best, with nothing but some tracks in the sand, partly blown over by the wind, to guide him ; but suffice it to say he was correct, which we ascertained two months afterwards; the horses and mules having been stolen from the neighbourhood of Fort Belknap, and a detachment of dragoons having been sent out after the marauders. Such is the force of habit, and most invaluable is this power in a country where stock is liable at any hour to be stolen.

The first specimen of the chapparal cock was here seen. It is a species of cuckoo, about as large as a grouse ; runs very fast, and will not fly unless closely pursued. It is the only bird that will attack the rattlesnake, which it does with great fury, seizing it by the neck and beating it to death with its short strong wings.

We gave chase to this specimen, a full grown male, but he escaped us by taking to the thick tangled bushes on the bank. Shortly after we came to the Big Witchita.

The bed of the stream was very wide, but there was but little running water in it, and that salt and bitter, disappearing frequently entirely in the sand, the shores frosted with deposits of salt and gypsum. We crossed and recrossed it several times during the afternoon, as it was very crooked and marching in a direct line, we had it in sight for a long

13*

distance, and it ran at right angles to our course every mile or two. The bed of the stream near shore was all quicksands, and every time we crossed more or less accident occurred, happily none serious.

My horse sank to the haunches in one instance, and in his plunges threw me off, but as the landing was soft, a plentiful bedaubing of red clay and mud was all the injury I received. Our horses and mules suffered very much from this service. Every plunge was made with a groan, and the strain upon legs and loins was very perceptible afterwards.

For many miles along the north shore, extended a meadow a mile wide, which in the rainy season must be entirely submerged, from the water marks, making a broad lake, where now no water could be seen, the grass very thin and coarse, like that in salt marshes. In crossing this, the Captain shot a doe, and we had a specimen of the dexterity and rapidity with which an Indian can skin a deer and prepare it for transportation. I timed Jacobs during the operation, and he was just *fifteen minutes* from the time the deer was shot until he had it prepared and packed on a mule.

The south shore now began to be bounded by a range of high bluffs. and hoping to find water there, we crossed at the first opening and bivouaced on top of a bluff, one hundred feet above the stream, giving us a level plateau, with grass for our animals and a good place to keep look-out for Indians.

In a ravine, a quarter of a mile off, Conner dug into the bank and found water, slightly impregnated with salt and gypsum, but cold, so spreading our blankets and picketing our animals, we prepared for the night on this eyrie.

The clear salt waters inviting us, we all descended for a bath, when just as we were " sans culotte," a succession of yells and shouts from the Indians, and the crackling and smoke from the dry grass, proclaimed a fire on top. Hastily ascending, we found our bivouac in flames, but baggage safe, except that of the Indians, who lost considerable.

We succeeded in beating out the fire, with blankets and horse cloths, and moving a little higher up, spent the most charming night of our trip, cool and free from insects, with a sky above as clear as sky could be, and countless meteors, coursing their way over the Heavens, principally from the north-east.

The twilight in this country is remarkable, prolonging the evening until a very late hour, and, when the sky is perfectly clear, lingering on the verge of day-break. On this night it was singularly so, and at no time between sunset and dawn, was it dark enough to obscure an object at one hundred paces distant. We made, this day, a march of forty miles.

July 30th.—Daylight found us all ready for moving, and passing through a meadow, below the bluff, where Jacob shot a monster rattle-snake, with nine rattles, we met with, in about an hour, the first gypsum, *in bulk*, we had yet seen.

The whole earth was covered with conical and rhomboidal chrystals of the mineral, whilst around and among it, lay jasper, agate and chalcedory, with some cornelian. Specimen hunting employed us for a short time, and many choice ones were found.

The stream—which we kept in sight of as much as possible—was still very crooked, and crossing and recrossing it very often during our march we found some land good enough to grow trees of a considerable size, but the most part was a barren waste covered with gypsum, with here and there the low stunted white cedar and patches of very thin coarse grass. In the fertile spots grew the China tree, the live oak and the mesquite, but all bearing marks of very insufficient nourishment from the soil. The same danger and difficulty from quicksands attended every crossing of the stream, and the bed—where dry—was invariably covered with a thick powder of gypsum mingled with salt.

Heat and exhaustion—thermometer one hundred and six degrees—compelled us to stop at noon and remain until next day.

We bivouaced upon a branch of the river, where was a spring icy cold, but intensely bitter. Not being able to find any other, we made a virtue of necessity and drank as little as possible, except in coffee, when the taste is somewhat disguised.* The Doctor made some lemonade with citric acid and oil of lemon, which refreshed us somewhat, but the *medicine* was too powerful to be mastered by ordinary means.

* It is well to remark, that our water-bags were filled and carried with us in case we should be unable to find any water at all, either sweet or bitter— which we had every reason to expect, and the supply of course remained untouched, fearful that such a contingency would arise.

A doe and fawn, killed by the incomparable Wagon, afforded us a savory meal, cooked Indian fashion, and our minds were diverted for a time by some very large bear signs in the sand, which we followed some distance, but unsuccessfully. Some anecdotes related by the Indians of the instinct and sagacity of bears, were very interesting. They say the animal invariably goes some distance with the wind, away from his first track, before making his bed to lie down— should an enemy now approach he is obliged to come with the wind, when the bear's acute sense of smell warns him in time to make his escape. When pursued he will sometimes take refuge in a cave, and should the hunter endeavor by building a fire at the mouth to smoke him out, he not unfrequently will advance, beat out the fire with his fore feet and then retreat into the cave.

Another anecdote, however, would seem to prove the bear correspondingly stupid. When the hunter cannot succeed in smoking him out, he sometimes descends into the cave with his rifle and a lighted torch. When the bear sees the light approaching he will sit upright upon his haunches, cover his face with his paws, and remain so until shot.

The black bear is harmless, unless wounded or accompanied by its young, when it is very dangerous to attack it.

I found a large species of wild gourd trailing on the ground, and very full of the vegetable, and caught a grasshopper as large as a good sized sparrow.

We noticed that insect life was very sparse in this region,

a great satisfaction to us, heat and bitter water being evils enough at one time.

Diarrhœa had now set in with most of the party, and all began to wear an anxious look.

Our course to-day was west of north, and distance thirty-five miles.

July 31st.—At six A. M., we left our bivouac, and taking a trail through the cedar brakes, and travelling up the river ten miles, we came to where it divided into three prongs.

Following the first, led us up a steep bluff to an elevated prairie, when a beautiful view was presented. In our rear the valley of the Big Witchita could be traced for many miles, in front, and to our right, the head waters, all emanating from the same barren and desolate hills of gypsum; In fact, the whole country here is one mass of gypsum, and is entirely uninhabitable.

We had seen but few Indian signs, nor do I believe they ever do more than pass through this region, as grass, water and game are all scarce.

With no regret, we bid adieu to the scene behind us, heartily wishing it might never be our lot to visit it again, and turning south after a ride of six miles, came to a tiny spring, trickling from an overhanging shelf of lime-stone.

Making a basin to receive the water, canteens and tin cups were soon busy, and from the number of cupsfull that found their way down our throats, in rapid succession, our thirst and joy at finding this God-send was very clearly evidenced. We also renewed the water in our bags, which we took care to do at every opportunity.

Near this spring, and on the highest point of the hill, was a Camanche grave, marked by a pile of stones and some remnants of scanty clothing. Conner pronounced it to be the grave of a woman, recognizing it as such by the few shreds of cloth, fluttering on a mesquite tree near the grave.

We now passed rapidly on in a southern course, and entered an extensive plain covered with thin coarse grass and stunted mesquite timber.

We moved parallel to a chain of mountains, making quite a variety to the dull monotony of the barren prairie, and striking the gypsum formation again halted towards sunset upon a branch of the Brazos, where we had bitter water, but plenty of grass and wild rye for our animals.*

Previous to reaching our bivouac, we crossed a narrow ridge, upon the top of which was the dry bed of a stream, which overflowing in time of high water, caused a most luxuriant growth of grass on the flats at either side. It reminded me of the course of the Mississippi.

Near this, one of the men got astray (in the tall coarse sedge, reaching higher than a man's head on horseback, and extending for half a mile on either side of the ridge) but with a succession of yells and shouts aroused the ever ready

---

* We occasionally passed oases of this kind in our trip, but so small was their extent, in proportion to the immense territory traversed, that they were more tantalizing than useful.

Wagon, who was scouting in the vicinity, and soon put him right.

Our bivouac was in a grove, the ground of an old Camanche camp* at the base of a succession of low hills of red clay, posted and sparkling with crystals of gypsum.

The timber was cotton wood and hackberry; the bed of the stream one quicksand, so that the animals were watered with difficulty.

An incident occurred here which shows how good a sentinel a horse or a mule is. They were all tied close to camp and we lounging on our blankets, when just at dusk the Major observed them start suddenly, with ears pricked, and one of them gave a loud snort. "Look out, something there !" was his sharp, quick exclamation. Instantly, every man was upon his feet, revolver and rifle in hand, when it proved to be one of the men who had gone over to put out the cook's fire on the gypsum hills, where it had been built for safety.

This incident shows also how prairie life sharpens the faculties of both men and animals. Distance to-day, thirty miles.

August 1st.—Our course to day was still south, towards some high knobs seen in the distance.

We left the gypsum formation and crossed a pretty extensive plain, but soon we struck it again and crossed a

---

* It was surprising how readily and with what accuracy in detail our Delawares would designate the tribe, the number and the disposition of the Indians, who had occupied the deserted camps we met with during our whole trip, and as we met with some of the same parties afterwards, their sagacity in this respect was fully established.

branch of the Brazos, the bed damp and oozy, with the water welling up through the sand at every step of our animals. We moved down the bed of the stream some distance, then took the shore, and came upon a very broken country, beyond which was a short prairie where was a prairie-dog village. These little creatures, so curious a feature in a prairie tour, gave us great amusement as we passed, sitting upon the mounds by their holes, frisking around or scuttling along from one hole to the other, filling the air with their low whining bark, and upon our approach throwing a summer-sault into their holes.

A short distance brought us to a branch of the Brazos, very deep, as clear as crystal, and filled with catfish, gars and buffalo fish, where we nooned, dining upon some of the fish cooked by the Major. Wagon caught a catfish four feet seven inches long, and nine inches across the head.

The blue and white cranes were seen here, also the yellow-legged snipe, and a species of large grasshopper of a shining black color, some of the specimens six inches long.

The grass was very rank and tall, and a high wind arising set it on fire from *our kitchen*, so that we had to make a hasty retreat up the steep bank on the opposite side of the creek, which we have called *Catfish Creek*. It was timbered with hackberry and cottonwood.

The bitter water here began to show its effects upon our horses. All were restless, and mine was affected with cramps, causing him to lie down and roll upon the ground in great

14

agony.   I was obliged to change him for one of the led horses
an impatient, nervous creature, who in crossing gave me *fall
the second* in the quicksands along shore.

On the top of the bank we struck a Camanche trail, very
broad, and made by the lodge poles, which they transport
from place to place in their wanderings by fastening them on
each side of their pack horses, leaving the long ends trailing
upon the ground, giving the trail very much the appearance
of a carriage road, in so much so that one of our party
remarked—without thinking that these lords of the plains
were obliged to eschew carriages of any kind—that "we must
soon overtake them, for here was the track of the chiefs'
travelling carriage," an idea that caused much merriment.

The country was now broken and rugged in the extreme
for some miles, and until we came to the plain, upon the
western border of which stood the singular knobs we had
seen in the distance.   One of these knobs—at the base of
which we passed — particularly attracted our attention.   It
rose several hundred feet above the surface in alternate
terraces of gray limestone, the whole forming a bell-shaped
mound, perfect in outline, and a landmark to the traveller for
a long distance.

Passing this range of knobs, we entered the most barren,
rugged and broken country we had yet met with, covered
with stunted mesquite trees and dwarf cedar, the ground
one mass of broken rocks.

Sunset found us toiling along, weary and half famished

for water. At length, we descended a ravine, and bivouaced "per force" near two pools of the most bitter water we had had to put up with. We now realized, how comparatively useless our gum-elastic water sacks were. The water not only became nauseous from the gum, but exposure to the sun rendered it equally unpalatable to the gypsum water.

We also had gum-elastic sacks for our rations of pork, and discovered that heat and grease together so softened this material, as to render it entirely unfit for service in that climate. The whole coating of gum peels off under such circumstances, and leaves the sack, not equal to one made of common canvass.

One or two *gutta percha* bags, unfortunately of small capacity, happening to have been brought along, their contents proved good, so that we fared better than could have been expected, but our miserable bivouac, for that night, will long be impressed upon our memories.

One of the soldiers, here became very violently ill with cramps and diarrhœa, and we were all suffering terribly and much exhausted by the constant doses of this most execrable stuff, impregnated, as it is, with sulphate of lime, sulphate of magnesia, sulphate of soda, chloride of sodium and hydrosulphuric acid,*

* Professor W. S Clarke, of Amherst College, made an analysis of this water, and gives the following as the result.

Water in fluid, ounces	.	.	.	.	.	.	4.000
Weight of Sulphate of Lime			.	.	.	.219
" " " Magnesia,			.	.	.088
" " " Soda,			.	.	.073
" " Chloride of Sodium,			.	.	.	.023
" " Hydrosulphuric acid,			.	.	.011

a most nauseous dose under any circumstances, but with the thermometer at one hundred and four degrees in the shade, and long rides in the hot sun, creating most insatiable thirst, our sufferings may be imagined but cannot be described.

I had my first experience here in mounting guard, which became necessary in the disabled state of our escort, both Indians and white men. We all had to take turns, and a wretched night passed in restlessness and anxiety. We made this day forty miles.

As may be supposed, we welcomed with joy the first streaks of day, and saddling up, we turned our back upon our wretched bivouac with alacrity, but apprehensive for the future. Ascending the steep banks of the ravine, we came upon a plain bounded upon the west by a most picturesque range of bluffs, then ascending and descending through hills, gullies, and ravines, we came, about eight, A. M., to the base of a mountain, which forming one of the range of bluffs mentioned, had attracted our attention for some time, glistening as it did in the sunlight. We ascended it and found its altitude, by barometer, *seven hundred feet* above the plain, and that it was composed of a *solid mass of gypsum*, the top level and covered with a dazzling white pavement of the mineral, as perfectly laid as though by the hand of man.

From our elevated position a magnificent panorama was spread out before us. In our rear, the rough and inhospitable country we had just left, with the fire from our lately burnt camp smoking in the distance, a fork of the Brazos, winding its tortuous and uninviting course at our feet, an extensive mesquite plain, with the bluffs which bounded the opposite shores of the Main Brazos, in the far back ground, whilst to our right could be seen the two conical peaks, which marked the source of the Brazos, towering towards heaven, and looking like two dim clouds in the distant horizon.

The view was truly attractive, but our sufferings for water overpowered all other feelings, and descending we pushed rapidly on, crossed the fork of the Brazos at our feet, and entered upon a plain covered with a singular growth of dwarf oaks bearing quite a large acorn, the oak a perfect tree in itself, but the highest not more than two feet high.

The soil now was gravelly, giving us hopes of soon finding water, but after a very long ride and much distress, we found nothing but a stagnant pool filled with vegetable matter and sickening to the taste. By boiling it in our camp-kettles and skimming off the green slimy scum, we managed to make coffee, and one of the Indians having shot a deer, we passed a comparatively comfortable night upon the open prairie.

We were surprised to find quantities of fish in this stagnant pool. Specimens of copper were also found, and fossil shells. We killed two rattlesnakes in our bivouac, and after filling our water-sacks with the boiled water, retired to our blankets, having in spite of our privations passed a very interesting

14*

day.*   Our course had been south, and distance forty-five miles.

August 3d.—We made an early start, still travelling south across the plain, which became more fertile at every step, covered with a rich growth of buffalo grass and very large mesquite trees—a great change from the land of bitter water.

Pretty soon we entered an extensive prairie dog town, where (the Doctor being anxious to procure one as a specimen) Conner and the other Indians made many shots, some of them effective, but did not succeed in securing a dog, as they tumbled into their holes and were lost. Two skeletons of heads were all that was obtained.

Enormous rattlesnakes were seen here, one of which the Major wounded, but it glided into a hole and could not be withdrawn. These reptiles are always found in numbers about these towns, where they subsist upon the puppies, as has been proven by opening a snake killed, and not as some suppose, living on friendly terms with the inhabitants.

A small species of owl, no doubt attracted by the same cause, was seen flying around, and rabbits running in and out of the holes, whether occuping those deserted by the dogs, or as one of the family, could not be ascertained.

The prairie dog is a species of marmot, with a head similar

* A good plan, when in a country like this, and having to drink such stagnant, warm and unpalatable water, is to cover a canteen or gourd with a piece of woolen cloth, or blanket, and filling the vessel, wet the outside and hang it on a tree or bush over night; by evaporation a cool drink is thus afforded at least once in twenty-four hours.

to a bull-dog puppy, the incisors like those of a squirrel, body about the size of a common rabbit, and tail like that of the chip squirrel.

The immense numbers of these animals in one of their towns, may be estimated from the fact, that we passed ten miles through this town, and allowing it to extend the same distance in other directions, we have an area of one hundred square miles, when by estimating the burrows at seven feet apart, the usual distance, and six dogs to a hole, we have a population not to be exceeded by any city in the world. They are found all over the far western prairies, from Mexico to the northern limits of the states, and always select the sites for their towns upon the most elevated lands, where there is no water, sometimes none for many miles, but where grows a species of short, wiry grass, upon which they feed.

This has induced many to believe that they do not require water, and as no rains or dews fall during the summer months upon these elevated plains, and the dogs never wander far from home, the conclusion is warranted that they require no water beyond what the grass affords. That they hybernate is evidenced from the fact that they lay up no store for the winter, and this grass dries up in the autumn.

The Indians say that they may be seen, towards the last of October, busy with weeds and grass, stopping up every passage to their burrows, and if they re-open them again before spring, mild and pleasant weather is sure to follow.

Usually, however, they never appear until settled weather in the spring, when they are about, as lively as ever.

We saw wolves frequently to-day, and a good many deer, which gave us cheering prospects for better times, nor were we disappointed, for shortly afterwards we struck the limestone and found a beautiful and abundant spring, bubbling up at the foot of an overhanging cliff, composed of limestone, a layer of gypsum over, conglomerate on top of that, and sandstone over all. Agate, chalcedony, jasper and cornelian abounded here in great quantity.

We nooned here, drinking copious draughts of this delicious water, which only he who has been so long deprived of it as we had been can fully appreciate.

Having refilled our water-sacks, we mounted again and crossed the south fork of the Brazos, finding the water undrinkable and the same appearance in the bed of the stream, the water disappearing entirely in the sand, and the shores frosted with salt and gypsum, the salt thick enough to be gathered in handsful.

We now found a very broken country, and after a short ride crossed another fork of the Brazos, which from a mountain which we ascended a short distance from the opposite shore, we called *Table Mountain Fork.*

This mountain was composed of calcareous sand-stone, rose precipitously from the plain and was quite level on top. Descending this, we crossed a succession of rocky bluffs, and finally ascending over a steep and dangerous road, came to a broad level plain, a spur of the Llano Esctacado, covered with buffalo grass and mesquite trees, and extending as far as the eye could reach in a perfect level towards the dim, cloud-like mountains at the head of the Brazos.* We found some deer here, and one of the Indians shot a fat doe.

* The Llano Esctacado, or staked plain, is the most elevated table-land on our continent, and is supposed to be the original level of the prairies East. The plain proper extends from the thirty-second to the thirty-sixth parallel of latitude, and is, in places, two hundred miles wide, without a tree or running stream throughout its entire surface.

Formerly a road was staked off across it by the old Mexicans for the use of traders, hence its name.

CHAPTER XII.

HEAD OF THE BRAZOS TO FLAT ROCK CREEK.

Halt on the Llano Esctacado.—Grand View.—Descend from the plain.—Long
Ride.—Miserable Bivouac.—Curious sight.—Panther Chase.—Terrible Storm.
—Severe sufferings.—Indian Shealing.—Pleasant dreams.—Water plenty.—
Singular bush.—Chain of lakes.—Beautiful spring.—Pleasant Bivouac.—
Mesquite Gum.—Kickapoos.—Fish shot.—Manner of spearing fish.—Reached
our Camp.—Move Camp.—Flat Rock Creek.

The Captain now stopped, to consult about going any
farther. We had achieved the main point in our trip and
were all heartily tired and disgusted with so inhospitable
a country, besides that, the sick man could barely support
himself upon his horse, and we all felt that to go any farther,
in uncertainty about water, was to peril the lives of the whole
party. We decided to return, and turning our horses heads
east, we commenced our journey back to camp over the plain
we had just reached.

A ride of six miles, brought us to a precipice bounding
this plain on the east, and with a sheer descent to the plain
below of six hundred feet. The view was the most extensive
and glowing in the sunset, the most striking that we had
enjoyed during our whole trip, combining the grandeur of
immense space—the plain extending to the horizon on every
side from our point of view—with the beauty of the contrast

between the golden carpet of buffalo grass and the pale green of the mesquite tree dotting its surface.

How to descend was now the question—nothing presented itself in the descent but a mass of loose rocks of white streaked limestone, no path ; no opening, the foot of white man never before had been here, but descend we must, so the first foot hold witnessed us, plunging, rolling and sliding—men, horses and mules, one after other, and sometimes on top of each other, pell-mell to the bottom.

I concluded to turn my horse loose and let him shift for himself, but came near losing him by the experiment. His rein caught upon a scrub cedar, and there he hung, like Mahomet's coffin, between heaven and earth, until fortunately another horse rolled against the tree, broke it off, and both came to the bottom together, safe except a few scratches.

When all had arrived at the bottom, Conner's first expression was, " now may be so, long ride to water," and so it proved, we rode until nine at night, the Captain and the Indians scouring the country in every direction, and found none, when, just as we were all in despair—the supply in our bags being so insufficient—a halloo in the distance, raised our spirits only to be again depressed.

It was Jacobs, who had found water in a small branch of Brazos, but on coming up, we found it so salt and bitter, that even our animals would not drink it.

We were too much exhausted to go further, so unsaddling, we prepared to pass the night and make out with the scanty store our water bags afforded us. Our miserable bivouac, was made more cheerful, however, by the delicious steaks of the fat doe killed in the afternoon, and now cooked by the Major in a style which would have done credit to a finished " cuisinier."

We supped heartily, and with hopes for to-morrow, rested as well as tired men could, with a yelping concert of wolves in their vicinity.

August 4th.—Long before daylight, we were off without breakfast, and riding rapidly and examining every spot where water might be thought to be, about eight o'clock we found in a branch, a small quantity of water, which though so putrid as to scent the atmosphere, our famishing animals drank greedily. We could not swallow it, though suffering terribly.

A curious sight presented itself here. Large numbers of buffalo fish, had penetrated to this point in high water, and their skeletons in thousands, lined the shores, where they had perished after the water receded, and afforded a rich repast for eagles and buzzards, whose feathers were thickly strewn around.

We pushed on, and about ten o'clock, the Captain surprised a panther, in his tracks—the first one we had met with —and giving chase, soon came to a fine stream, which from this circumstance, he called *Panther Creek*.

Joy at finding water, drove away all thoughts of the panther, and shouting out the welcome news, we were soon bivouaced under a wide spreading elm, enjoying good water

and a savoury breakast of venison and wild turkies, large flocks
of which abounded in the vicinity. The stream, was bordered
with hackberry, willow, wild china, post oak and elm, grass
very green and luxuriant, and being of course all much overcome, we rested here until three o'clock in the afternoon.

I found a large diamond back terrapin on the banks of the
stream, very similar to those found in the north; deer were
plenty, and many wolves.

Heavy clouds and the low rumbling in the west, betokened
a coming storm, just as we had got all ready to start, and
before we got far it burst upon us terrifically, with rain, hail,
thunder and lightning. A storm, on the plains, is a serious
matter. The wind blows irresistibly, and the driving rain and
hail so cuts and blinds both men and horses, that no headway
can be made against it. My horse turned completely round
in his tracks, and it was with much difficulty that I forced him
to the shelter of a low clump of bushes, where, dismounting, I
seated myself under their scanty cover, whilst he instinctively
turned and exposed his haunches to the blast, and stood with
drooping head and reeking flanks, trembling in every limb,
until its violence had passed.

Wet and uncomfortable, we started once more, but our
troubles were not yet over. We had, as we thought, left
forever the nauseous and disgusting water of the Brazos
country, and after our pleasant bivouac, were all refreshed
and cheered by the prospect of better times in our eastward
march to camp, when, after a long ride in our wet clothes, we

15

halted for the night, upon the banks of a fine running stream, and unsaddling, prepared for rest and repose, supposing of course, that the water was as good as that of Panther Creek, but oh, what a disappointment! Quite as bad in salt and gypsum as the waters of the Upper Brazos, this had the addition of more sulphur, and some rice cooked in it for the invalids, tasted precisely as if mixed with gunpowder; and to cap the climax the rain again began to pour down in torrents. We had to make the best of our situation, however, and to obviate the evils that beset us, with the means in our power.

We had taken no precaution to refill our water-bags at Panther Creek, feeling sure, as I before remarked, of finding plenty, but about *half a pint per man* remained in them, which tasted strongly of the gum, and having been heated and cooled several times, was a nauseous dose. With this we made some coffee, and building a fire under shelter of a bank, our Indians cooked a turkey, after their fashion. We then prepared quarters for the night.

A tent fly had been brought along, as an awning to noon under, and by stretching a lariat between two trees, we managed to make a triangular covering, open at both ends and just wide enough to hold our party, provided no man required more than his length and breadth to lay upon.

Under this we crept in our wet clothes, and many an impatient groan and exclamation, told how uncomfortable our quarters were, and how heartily we wished for morning.

Conner and the Indians went to work, and in an incredibly short space of time, constructed for themselves a most primitive but excellent protection for the night.

Selecting two small mesquite trees, growing near each other, they brought them together at top, to form the door, and then cutting poles, bent them in semicircles from the rear, all meeting in a point at the top, and covering this frame with blankets and horse-cloths, forming a fac simile of an old fashioned gig top, under which they all lay till morning. Our sick man was here so ill that we were in doubts about being able to get him to camp. We slept restlessly and only from sheer fatigue, our misery made more complete, by the attacks of musquitoes, gnats, &c., who, like ourselves, seemed to have sought shelter in our miserable tent.

I realized this night what I had often read of, viz. : the delicious dreams of water and cooling beverages, persons who are suffering from thirst experience. I fancied myself eating ice cream, Roman punch and sherbet, and revelled in their enjoyment, only to feel ten times more thirsty when I awoke.

August 5th.—Morning dawned upon us with a clear unclouded sky, and its first streaks found us on our eastward march, glad to find relief even in the motion of our horses from the sufferings of the night.

Much more rain had fallen in the section we reached after a ride of two hours, so that we began to find rain-water in all the holes and ravines we passed, and it is truly astonishing what a quantity of water the system can hold after a long deprivation ; canteen after canteen was emptied, and still whenever water appeared, each strove to be first to reach it, and equally so with our animals, their thirst seemed insatiable.

In crossing a ravine I found a curious bush, the leaf and stalk like the willow, with branches of balls on the limbs, similar to the sycamore, some green, some white, and others deep maroon, the different stages of the maturity of the plant. Conner said it was the button willow, a medical plant used by the Indians in cases of dysentery.

The plain was undulating and crossed at intervals by limestone ridges, timber mesquite ; the soil good and covered with a rich coat of buffalo grass.

We saw many deer and wolves, and about ten, A. M., came upon a chain of lakes, seven in number, the largest about three hundred yards long and twenty wide, the water clear and sweet, and filled with catfish and soft turtles.

Here we nooned, dining off some delicious catfish, cooked in the Major's best style, whose kindness, in this respect, throughout our dreary journey, can never fade from our memories.

We found the insects excessively annoying, which surprised us very much, as the banks of the lake were steep and rocky, and no marshy ground or mud in the vicinity, We were particularly annoyed by large black gnats, about the size of a common house-fly, and most inveterate blood suckers.

I may remark here, that on the head waters of the Brazos and Witchita, insect life entirely disappears, or at least is so sparse as to be scarcely noticeable, a natural consequence of the barren and desolate character of that region.

In the afternoon we changed our course north, towards the dividing ridge, between the Big Witchita and the Brazos. We crossed many fine limestone streams, and through the clear water, could see the bed of the streams, perfect pavements of large slabs of limestones, smooth and jointed, as if done artificially. This occurring in every case made it remarkable and worthy of note.

We reached the ridge and passed along the top, making a very long march, before we found, an hour after sunset, a most copious and beautiful limestone spring, which struck me so singularly that I have described it minutely.

In a gentle undulation of the prairie, on the eastern side of the ridge, we found this spring, rising out of the ground and enclosed on three sides by a rectangular wall about four feet high; at the narrowest part about six feet wide, and in length about ten feet; a small outlet emptied the overflow into an irregular pool, large enough to contain sufficient water for our thirsty animals, whilst we had the fountain for ourselves.

It was a surprise and almost like a dream, after the hard-featured country we had passed through, and our bivouac gave ample evidence of this cheering change in our circumstances, for to crown all, a bright full moon shone over us. We forgot fatigue, hunger and thirst, and a very late hour found us enjoying song, joke and conversation, until drowsiness

15*

overtook us in the midst, when, wrapped in our blankets, a few hours gave us refreshment for another ride.

During our afternoon march, a rattlesnake of a new species, as we thought, appeared in our path, and struck the Doctor on the sole of his boot, whilst on horseback. It was dispatched without ceremony, but in the hurry, so much mangled that we could do no more than take a general description of it. It was orange-colored on the belly, white ground and black marked in diamond upon the back, and had eight rattles. It was very vicious, making battle after it was badly wounded. This was the first time that any one of our party had come near a catastrophe from this source ; a lucky escape !

August 6th.—At sunrise we again ascended the ridge, and marching in a north-east course along the top, found large herds of deer. The soil very fertile, and mesquite timber larger than any heretofore met with. The Doctor, attracted by the large quantities of gum exuding from these trees, collected several pounds of it, which he intended to analyze.

The tree is beyond doubt a species of acacia, the gum having the same appearance and taste of the gum-arabic, and exuding in sufficient quantities to warrant its collection as an article of commerce, which would make a useful and profitable employment for the wandering Indians, if they could be induced to turn their attention to it.*

Soon the dividing ridge was found to be abruptly broken

* Since our return, an analysis has been made, and the report to the War

into a succession of bluffs, and a beautiful view spread before us. The Brazos in the distance, numerous short rocky bluffs, opening with vistas of mesquite flats, and our far off camp, which we were all so anxious to reach, lying in a clump of elms, at a distance of twenty miles, discernible from our elevated position.

We descended and wound through the openings in the bluffs for some miles, the soil very rich, grass and timber in abundance. until we came to a fine spring, shaded by a grove of button willow, near which was a Kickapoo camp of seventy lodges, making, with five to a lodge, three hundred and fifty souls.

They had just moved camp, and from the well-picked bones and lack of stench or scraps about, must have been on very short allowance.

A mile farther we struck a creek, winding its broad, clear stream over a flat rocky bottom, and abounding in fish and soft turtles, a most inviting place so much so, that the Captain, immediately decided to move over here as soon after reaching our camp as possible.

department, proves it to be equal to the gum arabic, envelopes having been sealed with it.

The subject of employing the Indians, in collecting this gum, was seriously entertained by gentlemen on the frontier when we left, and no doubt the experiment will be made and with every probability of profitable success, as the immense quantity of mesquite trees in that region, cannot fail to afford an inexhaustible supply, besides, whereas now the gum only exudes, from accidental openings in the bark, a system of bleeding, similar to that pursued with the sugar maple, must produce corresponding results.

Here for the first time I saw fish shot from horseback. Whilst the Major's horse was drinking an enormous cat-fish made his appearance, and lay still long enough to receive a bullet from his famous revolver, which had done such good service in ridding us of rattlesnakes during our trip. Conner told me he had frequently seen the Witchitas, and other Indians, spear fish on horseback. Their plan was for two or three to ride into the stream, armed with their spears, and as one became tired another took his place, until after chasing the fish from hole to hole, they worried them down and speared them with ease. Farther south, the Indians take large quantities of the electric eel, in the following way:

The eel abounds in pools. A band of Indians, will drive their whole herd of horses and mules into a pool and keep them moving, the eels constantly striking their legs, until the supply of electricity is exhausted, when the fish becomes torpid and is easily taken. The philosophy of this is, that after a discharge of electricity from the fish, it requires some time for the electric function to restore itself to sufficient vigor to act with effect.

The crossing, at this creek, being composed of one solid slab of limestone, smooth and level, the Captain called it *Flat Rock Creek*.

We continued our course, very anxious to get to camp, as the sun was so intensely hot; thermometer one hundred and four degrees in the shade.

We crossed the Brazos and came to a very rough country, difficult to pass through, on account of briars and scrub oaks, and about one, P. M., reached our camp, ten miles from where we left it, the gentlemen in charge having moved to this point to get purer water, and were now encamped in a beautiful valley, surrounded by high bluffs, on one of which was a Camanche grave.

We found several cases of sickness in camp, and among the rest a bad case of black typhoid fever—the first severe case of any kind we had had since we had been out.

And now having finished our perilous trip into those unexplored and inhospitable regions, and returned once more to enjoy the few comforts we left behind us, but one opinion prevailed with us, viz.: that the dangers we encountered and the privations we suffered had not been in vain, establishing as they did the fact, that for all purposes of human habitation —except it might be for a penal colony—those wilds are totally unfit. Destitute of soil, timber, water, game, and everything else that can sustain or make life tolerable, they must remain as they are, uninhabited and uninhabitable.

Perhaps some use may be made of the mineral resources, but that will have to be done under a load of peril to life, that few will be willing to encounter, none to endure for any length of time. Our party certainly, having left them without regret, will never return to them, except in memory, and then in reminiscences too painful far to be pleasant.

August 7th.—We moved camp at dawn of day to Flat

Rock Creek, where the natural advantages formed for us by far the most inviting and pleasant resting place to recover from our fatigue and toil that we had had during our whole trip.

A grove of stately and gigantic elms lined the bank of the stream for a quarter of a mile. Under the trees grew a rich growth of wild rye. In front stretched a rolling prairie; our rear closed in and defended by the clear, deep waters of the creek.

In a semicircle in front, and springing from the two wings of camp, were parked our wagons to defend our front, enclosing a space in which to herd our oxen and tether our mules and horses. Under the trees were pitched our white tents, a bright moon shining over all. Such was our camp at Flat Rock Creek, a cozy picture of safety and comfort, which to us, the returned vagabonds of the wilderness, had even more of romance than our late bivouacs had of reality.

The stream was filled with catfish, eels and turtles. I caught three varieties of the latter, viz., the snapper, the soft shell and a black mud turtle, striped with yellow and red on the head, body and legs. Of these the soft turtle was best and more delicate than the green turtle, either in soup or fricasee. It has an oval, dorsal shell—hard in the centre, with a broad, soft rim. The umbilical shell is, like the green turtle, white. It has claws instead of flippers, but the most striking peculiarity is the head, terminated with a snout like a hog, about half an inch long.

The whole surface of the stream was dotted at intervals with these heads when the creatures came up to breathe, and as they bit readily at the hook, any quantity were taken.

The catfish and eels were of the most marvellous size and delicacy, so that our stay here was spent in feasting to our heart's content on food which did not require a hungry man to relish, but which to us was doubly sweet after the privations of the past.

August 8th.—We remained quiet all day, enjoying our cool, breezy camp, and with the exception of a row among the teamsters, ending in one being badly wounded and his antagonist tied to a tree in the sun, the day passed pleasantly, nor did we forget our usual evening concerts, now that the chorus was full.

We retired early to prepare for our march to the Clear Fork in the morning, where we expected to meet the Camanches, and anticipated an interesting time.

CHAPTER XIII.

AUGUST 9th.—We marched early and left our late pleasant
camp in flames behind us. The tall rye and rank grass
made a fierce and rapid conflagration, which for days afterwards we could trace by the smoke on the horizon.

The day proved most intensely hot, and to our disappointment water was very scarce on our route. About noon, a
pool of tepid water was discovered in a ravine, and as the
prairie had been very much broken, making hard work for
the oxen, many of which gave out, and one dropped dead,
the Captain concluded to halt and encamp until next
morning. We camped upon a hill very hot and dry, and had
scarcely got settled when the prairie took fire, and was
extinguished with difficulty, making warm work for a hot
day.

The contrast to our stay at Flat Rock Creek was far from
pleasant, but we had become so accustomed *to take it* (to use
a trite expression,) *rough and tumble,* that our spirits were

not much affected. We all seemed determined to enjoy the fat when we could get it, and to be happy when we had to put up with the lean.

Though deer were plenty and the Delawares kept our *larder* well supplied, still we passed an uncomfortable after-noon and a more uncomfortable night, as insects were nume-rous and annoying.

August 10th.—We marched at two A. M.—the prairie very rough, broken and almost bare of grass. Soon an accident occurred to the train, when Jacobs gave us a specimen of the nerve and reliability of the Indian upon his own powers and sagacity.

Our anxiety to hear from home and friends induced us at Flat Rock Creek, to prevail upon him to go into Fort Belknap, mail letters sent by him, and bring us what might be there.

Never having been in this country before, he would have to depend upon powers which, with Indians, seem to me to be instinct more than calculation. He consented to go, but proposed to march with us until daylight this morning. The accident detaining us some time, he became impatient, and suddenly wheeled his horse at a tangent, and grunting out, half in soliloquy, "May be so he too long," disappeared in the gloom, to our left. On the afternoon of the tenth day from this date, he made his appearance in our camp on the Clear Fork, seventy-five miles from this point, bringing our letters, papers, &c., from Fort Belknap, where he arrived on

16

the fourth day after he left us, having found his way there
and back through this trackless wilderness as true as the
needle to the Pole.   Surely, what life can be more calculated
to harden the frame and steel the nerves, than this one of
such bold self-reliance.

One of our Delawares, Jackson, amused us very much during
our ride.   He had always appeared to us demure and morose
in temperament, but to our surprise and amusement he broke
out with one of our camp-fire songs, which, requiring a good
deal of action, made it very ludicrous, the whole performance
proving to me my before-formed opinion, that the Indian is
far from being the non-observant creature he is supposed to
be.   The tone, the manner, and gesticulation of the original
of this song, were expressed, though somewhat in broad bur-
lesque, yet sufficiently accurate to prove a quick perception
of the ridiculous and close imitative powers.

Shortly after daylight we reached a deep, broad bed of a
creek, which requiring heavy work to bridge, we halted and
encamped.

Our amateur sportsmen started in pursuit of game, and
found the creek full of deep water, a mile below camp, and
plenty of catfish, gar, and soft turtle.

A new species of gar was seen here, of a deep, shiny black
colour, the shape, size, &c., the same as the grey gar.

About noon, Indians were seen approaching, and pretty
soon Ke-tum-e-see, a chief of the Southern band of Camanches
rode in, accompanied by two of his wives.   He told us that he

had been riding very hard and far to overtake us. He heard we were in the country, and endeavoured to persuade some of his band to visit us, but they were too lazy, so he determined to come alone, and had been six days on our trail, following it through a good portion of the Upper Brazos country, where, like ourselves, he came near perishing for want of water.

In addition, he gave us the *agreeable intelligence,* that a war party of two hundred and fifty northern Camanches, Apaches and Navajoes, had been hovering around us, between the Big Witchita and Brazos for two days.

They were on a foray to the frontier of Mexico, to take revenge for some of their bands, shot whilst on one of their marauding expeditions last year, and coming across our trail, followed it until reconnoitering and finding but *thirteen* in our party, they hesitated to attack us, feeling sure that a *large command* must be in the neighborhood, as they could not believe that so small a force of white men would venture so far into their fastnesses, unless supported at short distance by a large party—so that the order of things was reversed, in our case, and in our weakness, we found our immunity from annihilation.

We felt much obliged to them for their forbearance, and on questioning him further, found out the night when they were nearest us. It was the night when the gentlemen of the party were on guard, and we all had remarked how unusually restless our horses and mules were, a sure sign of danger near.

Ke-tum-e-see, was a fine-looking man, about fifty years old, full six feet high, with a dark red bronze complexion.

His wives—(these were two, and the youngest of four, whom he commanded) were mere children, the one about eighteen and the other not sixteen years old.

Both were pleasing in their appearance, but entirely different; the youngest being chubby and dark, the eldest lean and as fair as a quadroon. Whether it was by accident or from choice that the chief had made his selection, I know not, perhaps, a spice of both, though he gave us to understand he was quite an *epicure* in such matters.

An odd mixture of wealth and poverty, marked this trio. Ke-tum-e-see was dressed in corduroy leggins and buckskin moccasins, much worn, an old, torn, greasy, checkered cotton coat, and a sixpenny straw hat, whilst his bridle was ornamented with perhaps *fifty dollars worth of silver.*

His wives were attired in dark calico shirts, with leggings and moccasins in one piece, like a boot; their clothes thin, dirty and common, and heads bare ; the hair short, thick and uncombed, whilst their bridles were similarly ornamented as the chief's ; and the youngest, who appeared to be the favorite, wore in addition, a girdle studded with silver brooches, very heavy, showy and costly. The wives rode astride, driving the pack horses, who bore their scanty stock of cooking utensils, blankets, skins, &c., and as soon as they arrived, set diligently to work to unsaddle, unbridle and lariat the horses, and make from bushes and blankets a temporary shelter for their lord.

The chief threw aside his *riding dress* and came up to our tent to dine, " in puris naturalibus," except his red blanket. The only ornament or appendage he wore was a long tail of buffalo hair, depending from a bunch of eagle's feathers, fastened on the crown of his head, and reaching in a four-fold plait to the ground; a mark of his rank in the tribe. In eating, drinking and smoking, he appeared very abstemious, but this turned out to be " for the nonce." He wrote (or at least copied) our names, and told Conner, who was interpreter, to tell the captain, that when the sun went down, he wanted to talk.

In the afternoon the elder of the wives visited us and interested us very much by her simplicity and curiosity. A burning glass, compass and magnet were shown her, and her delight knew no bounds, until finally the old chief, either fearing she might learn too much, or from jealousy, ordered her away, in a short gruff tone, and retired himself to his shealing. At sun-down he returned for the talk. After a smoke he commenced, holding in his hand a bundle of short stalks of grass. Handing these, one by one, to the Captain, he made his remarks upon each, representing by each, one of the chiefs or war captains of his band, and giving his disposition towards the whites. After remarking upon four of high standing, and three of mediocrity, he bundled the balance, eight in number, in a bundle, and handed them together, with a grunt and remark, " no count." He then expressed himself as anxious to come into any measures pro-

16*

posed by Captain Marcy; swore eternal friendship for the whites, and ended by volunteering to return and induce his people, by all means, to meet us on the Clear Fork. Another smoke all round, and the talk closed; the chief went to his shealing, and we to repose, after our early start and hot day, —thermometer one hundred and four in the shade.

August 11th.—At one, A. M., we were on the march again, and moving very slowly on account of the roughness of the prairie.

Ke-tum-e-see and wives marched with us, intending to spend the day, and leave in the morning for the camp of his band.

Arriving at Double Mountain Fork of the Brazos, we found so much work to be done, in bridging, that orders were given to encamp.

The heat was intense, the thermometer, at nine A. M., one hundred and five degrees in the shade, the stream was full of fish and turtles, so that those who chose to brave the heat, had fine sport.

We saw but little of the chief and his wives, as they were resting all day. A general lassitude also pervaded our camp, from early rising, long marches and intense heat, so that the day passed quietly.

During our march, we found plenty of the *missletoe* on the Mesquite trees; we found limestone and iron ore in abundance, the timber, elm, mesquite, wild china, and post oak.

August 12th.—As early as usual we were in motion, and

passed the Double Mountain Fork, entering immediately, upon a very fertile region, alternately with mesquite flats and limestone ridges.

The chief and his wives, left us, in true wild Indian style "sans ceremonie." They had been riding in advance of the train, and suddenly wheeling to the right disappeared over a ridge, without turning to say good bye, or give any other signal of their intention.

The day was intensely hot, thermometer one hundred and six degrees, and we made a very long march, being anxious to get to the Clear Fork, for fear the Camanches if there, might get tired waiting, leave, and thus defeat our plans for them.

In crossing a limestone ridge, an extensive prairie, spread out before us, covered as far as we could see, with a very rank growth of sunflower, a sure indication of a rich soil. Crossing this with difficulty, for it was so thick and tall that we had to force our horses through it, we came suddenly upon the road from Belknap to Chadbourne, and marching in a northerly direction encamped about seven miles from the Clear Fork, near two pools of tolerable water.

On this prairie were some gigantic growths of the prickly pear. Some we passed were fifteen feet high and forty in circumference, of the broad palmated species.

In New Mexico, this plant is used as a most nutritious and excellent food for stock. It is cut with a hooked knife (made on purpose and fastened on a long handle,) and laid in layers with dry coarse grass between, the whole then set fire too, when a few minutes deprives the plant of its thorny prickles, and it is then eaten with great avidity by stock; an excellent substitute in a country where grass is so scarce.

Immense flocks of doves covered the plain, attracted by the seeds of the sunflowers, and we shot numbers for our mess table.

August 13th.—At an early hour we reached the Clear Fork, which, at the crossing, was about thirty yards wide, running through perpendicular rocky banks over a rocky bed, the water beautifully clear and the valley of the Clear Fork about a mile wide.

To our surprise, on ascending the opposite bank, the road wound through a large field of oats on one side and corn on the other, and in the distance, we saw a house, the first we had seen for near three months—it carried us back to home and friends. In this solitary spot, Colonel Stem, late Indian agent, established this rancho, about three years since. The corn and oats were put in with the labour of eight men, and by simply turning over a furrow with the plough, no necessity for harrowing or pulverizing. The crop sold, in the ground, for forty-five hundred dollars, a proof of the fertility of the soil.

The Colonel, on his return from his rancho in February, 1854, in company with a friend, was murdered by a wandering party of Kickapoos; they shot at them, but missing, clubbed their rifles and beat them to death, then stealing what was most valuable, made their escape. This occurred within ten miles of Fort Belknap.

The punishment of these murderers is an instance of the manner in which justice is done among these barbarous people. From information given by a boy who was with the Indians at the time the murders were committed, the commanding officer at Fort Arbuckle sent for the Kickapoo chiefs, and told them the murderers must be given up, at the same time a large reward was offered for their apprehension.

The chiefs told him that they had been in council all night upon the matter; that they knew the murders were committed by two of their band, who were absent on assembling the men of the tribe, and that they had sent their people out by threes in search, so that any person meeting one Kickapoo alone, or two in company, might immediately arrest him or them. In a short time one of the murderers was arrested by his own people, firmly bound, and placed on horseback to be taken into the fort. A short distance from that place, he managed to free himself from his bonds, and throwing himself from the horse attempted to escape, but was immediately shot down and his dead body carried in and delivered to the officer in command. The other made his escape, but after eluding pursuit for a time made his way to a village where his brother lived. Entering this, he commenced exclaiming in a loud voice, " I am the murderer of Colonel Stem, will no one take me and deliver me up for punishment ?" In this way he reached his brother's lodge, entering which, he said, " My brother, I committed this murder. I am tired of life. I am hunted down like a wild beast, and I want to die. I tried to join the Camanches, but would have starved to death before I could have found them." Food was set before him, of which he partook. His brother and he then walked out of the village, when the former said to him, "My brother, you have disgraced our tribe, and it is my duty to kill you. I have all along told you that your course of life would lead you to this, and however painful it may be to me, yet justice demands the sacrifice, I must kill you." Stepping behind him he then felled him to the earth with his tomahawk, and with repeated blows despatched him. A council was then held, at which the brother made a speech, stating what he had done, and why, ending by calling for a volunteer to behead the body and take the head into the fort, as the distance was too great and the weather too hot to take the whole corpse. No one volunteering, he then said, "I must do it myself," which he did, and carried the head to Fort Arbuckle, where it was buried. Such is Indian justice.

We passed the rancho and encamped about a mile below, intending to wait for the Camanches, who had not yet arrived.

Soon after encamping, Ke-tum-e-see again made his appearance. He said he had concluded not to take his wives with him, as it was uncertain where he should find his band, and they might have a long ride—*a rare instance of consideration in a wild Indian*. He left them in charge of Connor, and started in course of the afternoon.

Our camp was very convenient and picturesque. A level prairie, bounded on the west by a range of bluffs, extended for about six miles in length and half a mile wide.

We were encamped on the eastern edge, about one hundred feet above the Clear Fork, between which and us was a low valley, shaded by noble pecan and elm trees, where the mess fires were lighted, and the Delawares made their camp.

The prairie was destitute of timber, but very breezy, and free from insects.

Our wagons were parked in a large semicircle in front, and with the valley and river in our rear, we were secure from attack. A large and cool spring percolated from the bank a short distance below our camp, and, with the fish and turtles from the stream, we had a very good time during our stay, which was a long one.

Several deserted camps were scattered over the valley, showing this to be a favourite spot with the wild Indians, and, in roaming around, I picked up beads and other relics.

The stream afforded delightful bathing ground, which we availed ourselves of during our stay, and could now roll up in our blankets at night, with the comfortable assurance of no more early starts and long rides, under that blazing sun, for some days—a great relief, with the thermometer averaging one hundred and four degrees daily, the nights, as usual, always pleasant, and seeming as if made for sleep.

CHAPTER XIV.

AUGUST 14th.—When Major Neighbours sent out runners
to the Camanches, he intimated to them the plans of the
government, and they in reply expressed their wish to be settled upon the Clear Fork, as it was their old hunting and win-
tering ground. Ke-tum-e-see having corroborated this state-
ment—preparations were immediately made to explore in the
vicinity of camp, but about ten, A. M., just as the party were
about to start, two sub-chiefs of Se-na-co's band rode in to
hold a talk. Their names were Qua-ha-we-tah, or tall tree,
and Oti, or hunting a wife. The latter was by birth a Tonkaway, but was taken prisoner by the Camanches when a child;
he had adopted their habits and tribe, and become a chief
among them. Both were tall, powerful, athletic men, very
savage in their appearance, scantily dressed, and fully

painted. They rode into camp bareheaded, with *umbrellas* hoisted, an incident which occasioned some merriment.

Previous to holding the talk, they improved their toilette, when I perceived what gave Oti his more than usually diabolical appearance, which I could not account for before on account of the load of paint with which his face was covered. Producing a small looking glass and a pair of rude tweezers, which he used with great dexterity, he proceeded to pull out every hair he could find upon his face. His hair on his head was cropped close, except the crown tuft, from which depended his buffalo hair plait, and commencing at the roots of the hair on his forehead, he pulled out eyebrows, eyelashes, beard, &c., and then smearing the whole with yellow clay, streaked his eyelids with vermillion, spotted his cheeks with the same, and finished by daubing his chin with black, making a most hideous specimen out of himself in a very short time The other was not so particular, but with his matted hair, hooked nose, and wide mouth, was ugly enough without any effort to increase it.

They held their talk, and told us that we must not believe Ke-tum-e-see, that he was a liar and a scoundrel, and that they would go off and bring in Se-na-co, who alone was authorized to speak for the tribe; they said the tribe was friendly, and would accede to the proposed settlement. Rations were then served to them, and they passed the night under the trees in the valley, intending to leave early in the morning.

In the course of the afternoon Oti asked me for some sugar from the dish standing on our camp-table; and as our stock was small, I took out several large lumps and offered them. He shook his head and walked off, apparently angry. Pretty soon he returned, and pointed again to the dish. I nodded my head, and he deliberately poured the whole into his bag. The same thing happened with their rations; they refused them, and the commissary-corporal immediately reported the case to the Captain, who told him to double them; this was done, and they took them at once.

August 15th.—On coming out this morning, I was surprised to find the chiefs still lingering around camp, although having saddled up their horses. I found out that they had seen some whiskey and wanted to get it. Both were armed with bows and arrows in addition to their rifles. I tried to barter for a bow, quiver and arrows, offering goods and money to much more than their value, but no, they would trade for nothing but whiskey, and upon my offering it, (which I did to try them,) were willing to give their bows and arrows for a bottle full.

Conner told me that this was their way, if they want anything, they must have it, let it cost what it will. He said he once got a mule, which he afterwards sold for *fifty dollars*, for a *plug of tobacco*, and, as I have observed before, I could readily have got the two bows, quivers and arrows, for a *short quart of whiskey*. They care nothing about money, as they cannot use it, all they think of is the gratification of their appetite, even if this, as in this instance, should cost them the very means by which they sustain life. As I would not give them the whiskey, they mounted and rode off looking very glum and disappointed.

Conner told me that it was but a short time since the Camanches would drink whiskey, always refusing it and saying that it made fools of them and they did not like it, but a colony of Germans settled upon the upper waters of the Canadian, and from frequently visiting them the appetite has been acquired by occasional indulgences, and now is quite prevalent among them.

He related a strange tale connected with this German settlement, which although savoring so much of the marvellous, I am obliged to believe, from his earnest asseverations of its truth, and my own observations upon the character of the wild Indians.

Shortly after the German emigration, a wild Camanche who had never seen them, met one in the prairie. The German wore his full beard, which with his hair was long and shaggy. Surprised at this unusual sight, the Indian shot him and skinned his *whole head*, the skin having been afterwards found in his possession, preserved and shown as a specimen of an unfound race of men.

Notwithstanding this bloody stretch of curiosity, Conner said that the Germans and Indians lived on terms of great amity, the former treating them with great hospitality whenever they visited the settlement, and a very straight road to a wild Indian's heart is through his stomach, as they are always ready to eat and drink.

August 16th and 17th were spent in explorations to find a suitable tract to be surveyed for the location of the Camanches, and finally one was selected about three miles farther up the stream from our camp, comprising every essential of upland and meadow, with fine water and timber, the amount of land necessary being six square leagues.

August 18th.—Se-na-co and his party arrived to-day. He was very prepossessing in his appearance, about five feet eight inches in height, not stout, but his frame firmly knit, very dark complexion, with a countenance mild but decided. He dressed without any ornament, and in this respect was a great contrast to his followers.

With him came Qua-ha-we-ti and Oti, the chiefs who had previously visited us, and Naroni, *or little piece of meat thrown over a pole*, and Straight-fellow, two war captains, besides a large party of warriors, women and children.

A very interesting woman accompanied this party. She was the widow of San-ta-na, a celebrated chief who died about three years since, and still mourned her loss, going out every evening in the neighborhood of camp, to howl and cry and cut herself with knives, according to the custom among them of persons in affliction. She had separated herself in a measure from the tribe, and formed a band of women, seven in number, like herself widows. She owned a large herd of mules and horses, and was a most successful hunter, having alone shot with her rifle fifteen deer in a morning's hunt. She was a fine looking woman, an Amazon in size and haughty bearing, rode astride, and dressed in deep black.

There was an invalid in the party, a chief, crippled with rheumatism and disease of the spine, drawn into a sitting posture by his ailments, emaciated to a skeleton, and a most pitiable sight, particularly distressing to us from our knowledge of the hardships and privations suffered by them in their wandering life.

The poor creature was perched upon a rude contrivance of sticks lashed on a horse, and bolstered with bags of grass, with a blanket and circingle passed over and around the whole to keep him steady, and having the feeble use of his hands, he guided the horse without assistance. A rude litter accompanied him, upon which he could ride during heat and exhaustion. This was constructed by lashing long poles to either side of a mule, leaving the ends trailing upon the ground. Cross sticks were lashed upon the trailing ends, and skins slung to these made the bed, and by the addition of two poles bent in semicircles and fastened diagonally over the bed, a shelter from the sun was made by covering them with green branches.

He had a *slave* to lead or drive the mule and lift him back and forth. This was a boy about sixteen, a Mexican, taken prisoner in some foray, dressed and painted like an Indian, and apparently quite reconciled to his degraded life, the

17*

whole forming a wretched picture of misery and poverty, mixed with considerable ingenuity and contrivance.

Naroni rode in in grand costume. He wore an old blue military coat, with tarnished epaulettes, and covered with bullet buttons, a wampum necklace, almost equal to a breastplate, numerous ear-rings, finger-rings, and a large ring in his nose, completely encircling his mouth, and bright red leggins.

But his crowning glory was his head-dress. From the crown of his head started out four long eagle's feathers, two on each side. To the centre was attached his buffalo hair plait, studded, at intervals of an inch or two, with enormous silver medallions, of an oval shape, and at least four inches in largest diameter. This plait swept the ground, and he seemed to set great store by it, as nothing would induce him to part with one of the ornaments. A rifle and bow, quiver and arrows, completed his costume and equipments; but being slender in figure and short in stature, his appearance was not at all imposing.

Straightfellow was very miserably clad, dirty and ragged, with a very forbidding countenance, indicative of cunning and cruelty.

The women were ugly, crooked-legged, stoop-shouldered, squalid and dirty, with haggard and prematurely old countenances, their hair cropped close to their heads, and with scarce a rag to cover their nakedness.

They led, or drove off, the pack-horses and mules into the valley, and soon all was life and bustle—some cutting down green limbs to construct their temporary shelter, some building fires, cooking, &c., and others unsaddling, unpacking, watering and tethering their animals.

Some of the visiters made their shealings on the prairie above us, so that, in a little while, we were surrounded by these wild creatures. Among these was a warrior armed with a lance and shield. The lance was a long, straight piece of steel, about two feet and a half long and an inch wide, tapering to a point. This was fixed into a slender handle of bois d'arc, about four feet and a half long, making the weapon seven feet in length; the handle ornamented with tufts of coloured cotton yarn and strips of cloth worked with beads.

The shield was round, and about two feet in diameter, made of wicker-work, covered first with deer skins and then a tough piece of raw buffalo-hide drawn over, making it proof against arrow-heads. It was ornamented with a *human scalp*, a grizzly bear's claw and a mule's tail, significant of the brave warrior and successful hunter and horse-thief, and the fastenings for the arm were pieces of cotton cloth twisted into a rope.

During their stay, we endeavoured to get this man to show us his exercise with these weapons, but he peremptorily refused, and this I understood is universal with them, a proof of their cunning.

These Indians had plenty of horses and mules, but generally a very inferior stock, the rest of their camp material was meagre and scanty in the extreme.

August 19th.—The first thing wild Indians ask for on coming into camp, is something to eat, they are always ready and consume large quantities.

The Captain had an ox killed for them this morning, and the women were soon busy in preparing it for present and future use. Every edible part was consumed, even the entrails, which are considered a choice delicacy, were drawn through the coals and devoured, reeking with excrement.

The women boned the flesh and then split it, haggling and carving it into long chains of lumps and then throwing it over poles, dried it in the sun, when it looked like links of stale sausage. The caul, suet, and other inside fat, were dried whole, and the cannon bones and hoofs first scorched before the fire and then hung up in the sun.

The portions of meat intended for present use, were prepared by placing them upon a rude scaffold over a slow fire, in the same way as previously described among the Kickapoos, and which I have seen done by the frontier squatters. It dries the meat, without depriving it of its juices, and prevents decomposition. A supply of corn from the rancho above us, together with some coffee and sugar, capped the climax of their happiness, and their bivouac wore a very cheerful appearance during the day.

The men of the party spent the day in painting themselves and lounging in their shealings, or wandering listlessly from tent to tent, expressing either surprise or pleasure by a grunt or a grin.

The intense heat—thermometer one hundred and six degrees—caused them to denude themselves entirely, except the breech-cloth, so that with the yellow, black and red paint, they presented a motley appearance.

They parted their hair from the centre of the forehead back to the crown, and made a streak of yellow, white or red, along the divide, a custom in which they were greatly assisted by large beds of yellow and white clay, which they discovered in the valley some distance down the stream. I could not discover whether each had a distinct style of daubing himself, but suppose this to be the case, as all were different.

A fat, chubby faced warrior, painted a fac simile of a *saw* around his jaws in black, his cheeks red, his eye-lids white, and his forehead and divide of his hair yellow, smearing his body also with yellow.

The invalid painted his face red, his eyelids white and streaked his face with black, like a ribbed nose babboon. Another painted one side black and the other yellow, continuing the process down to his waist. Another daubed yellow on one side and red on the other, his eyelids white and streaks of black upon his cheeks, in imitation of snakes. The boys also painted themselves; and several of the women had cheeks and hair stained with red. In short, all that savage fancy could do to increase savage ugliness was done, and a more diabolical, and at the same time ludicrous set, it would be hard to meet with.

About nine at night several of them collected upon the prairie to sing and dance. Seated on the ground in a circle, the leader commenced drumming upon a tin mess pan, accompanied with a low, guttural, monotonous chaunt, at intervals raising his voice louder, when a general grunt or a yell was added by the rest, and the whole strain ended with a prolonged *ugh*.

They sung for more than an hour, occasionally two or three throwing their arms up and hopping around like what children call playing at frogs, ending by seating themselves again with a grunt.

I soon tired of the scene, which by the light of a low fire looked more like a parcel of monkeys at dull play than any thing else. Their audience of teamsters and soldiers, however, seemed greatly pleased, and as a novelty it was somewhat interesting.

August 20.—The usual morning toilette was gone through with by the men, but the intense heat—one hundred and five degrees in the shade — kept all quiet in and about camp, except the women, some of whom were unusually busy, conspicuous among whom were the two wives of the chief Ketum-a-see.

Our Delawares took the opportunity to have their deer skins—of which they had accumulated quite a large bale—dressed by these women, and the process was very simple but rapid. Having soaked the skins thoroughly, they threw them over a smooth log leaned against a tree at an angle, and then taking a rib of a deer in both hands, removed the hair by scraping it against the grain; they then stretched and dried them, when they became beautifully soft and white. To color them, they tied several into a chimney shape, hung to a limb, and building smoulder fires under them they soon changed to yellowish brown on the hair side, and light yellow on the flesh side.

Great apprehensions were entertained that Ke-tum-e-see had been waylaid and murdered, as he was absent so long, but about noon he rode in, and gave as a reason for his delay that he had spent the time in endeavoring to persuade his followers to come in, but without success. His two wives ran to meet him, and seemed quite overjoyed at his arrival, most probably because he had left them entirely among strangers, as I cannot imagine any affection in the case.

At dusk the chiefs were assembled in council, and seated on the ground around the light of candles and lanterns, pipes were smoked, and Captain Marcy addressed them, through Conner, the interpreter.

Captain Marcy told them "that he had seen their Great Father in Washington, and he had sent him out to locate and survey lands for them, that they might have homes and learn to cultivate the soil and no longer lead the uncertain life they did; that buffalo had disappeared from these plains and deer and other game were fast disappearing; that in a few years they and their children would have to resort to some other means than the chase for a subsistence; that they would not be permitted to depredate upon the white settlements, and there was no alternative—they must learn to cultivate the soil.

He told them "that their Great Father would send them agricultural implements and seeds, also men to teach them to farm, and that he would provide for them until a crop was raised. That he — Captain Marcy — had been among tribes in the North, who once lived as they were living, but who, on advice, had learned to cultivate the soil, and were now living like the whites, with plenty to eat and wear. That if they would do as their Great Father wished them, they would have reason to thank him in a few years. That an agent would be sent to reside among them, and with the assistance of the United States' troops would see that they were not molested by white men, or other wild Indians if they remained friendly.

Se-na-co rose and replied, speaking in a slow, distinct and impressive tone, using but little gesticulation, but repeatedly placing his hand upon his heart. He said, "The chiefs and head men of the Southern Camanches have authorized me to reply to the talk which our Great Father has sent us by our friend, Captain Marcy.

"What I am about to say will be straight-forward and the truth, and the sentiment of all my people.

"We remember what our former chief, Mo-ko-cho-pe told us before he died, and we endeavor to carry out his wishes after he is gone.   He visited our Great Father at Washington, and brought us a talk from him.

" He told us to take the advice and example of the whites, and it would make us happy and benefit us.

" We are glad to hear the talk which has been sent us at this time ; it makes our hearts warm, and we feel happy in knowing that our Great Father remembers his poor red children on the prairies.

" We accept this talk, and will endeavour to accede to all our Great Father requires of us.

" I am pleased to see our friend, Captain Marcy, once more. I well remember seeing him five years since, near this very place, when I stayed over night with him, and have often inquired of the whites I have met, what had become of him, and I was much pleased when I was told he was to meet us here."

He stopped, seated himself, and many questions were put to him, which he answered freely and favourably.

All this time Ke-tum-e-see sat like a statue, glum and silent, evidently displeased at not having been spokesman.

Although he and Se-na-co expressed themselves anxious to meet the views of the government, they were evidently afraid of their followers, and we anticipated that much perplexity might arise from this cause.

The presents—consisting of printed cottons, handkerchiefs, blankets, knives, stroudding for leggins, armlets of silver, long

18

wampum beads, paint, &c.,—were now handed in bulk to the chiefs, and, after another smoke, the council closed.

August 21st.—This morning the chiefs distributed the presents, and great delight was manifested, particularly among the squaws, who kept up a continuous chattering.

It requires a good deal of knowledge of Indian fancies to select presents with judgment. Different tribes have different tastes. The northern Indians like gay clothing and blankets, ear-rings, brooches and beads of bright colours. The Camanches prefer dark clothes and heavy silver armlets, and long wampum beads, both the latter being very expensive, particularly the wampum beads, which are to be procured but in one place, a small town in New Jersey.*

Our stock of presents was very well selected, so that all were pleased and spent the rest of the day in painting and bedizening themselves, making many a funny show.

I surprised a party of women whilst they were bathing in the stream at mid-day, or rather they surprised me, as they bathed along side of the road and in sight of camp. I observed, however, that they showed great dexterity in avoiding unnecessary exposure. Wrapping blankets around themselves, they entered the stream where a tree or bush

---

* Wampum is made of the thick and blue part of sea clam-shells. The thin covering of this part being split off, a hole is drilled in it, and the form is produced and the pieces made smooth by a grindstone. The form is that of the cylindrical glass beads called bugles. When finished they are strung upon small hempen cords about a foot long. In the manufacture of wampum from six to ten strings are considered a day's work.

stood or hung convenient for them to place their blankets on so soon as they were immersed, and thus avoided exposure almost entirely.

The Camanches are very fond of bathing, both men and women, but cleanliness is only partially promoted by it, as they are either unable or neglect to change their clothing, but wear it in a filthy state.

The women observed the same modest caution in mounting their horses. They rode astride, and like all Indians mounted upon the right side of the horse. Drawing the left foot up, after placing the right in the stirrup, they extended it over the saddle at right angles to the right, instead of describing the arc of a circle, performing the feat and seating themselves with much ease and grace. This fact was common to all the females we met.

Towards sunset I observed one of the Chief's wives leading a horse and mule slowly backwards and forwards through a slow fire, which scattered over quite a large bare spot of ground, made a dense white smoke without flame, and at the same time I was sensible of an aromatic perfume proceeding from the valley. Upon inquiry, I found it was the process of hardening the hoofs by exposing them to the smoke and vapour of the wild rosemary—artemisia—large quantities of which grew in the valley of the Clear Fork.

August 22d.—A little Mexican made his appearance among the Indians this morning, dressed in a gay dressing-gown and pantaloons, and was immediately recognized by the Captain as a worthy he had seen during his Red River trip among the Witchitas. At that time, the Captain asked him why he did not leave the Indians and go home among his own people. He replied, "Me bin so long mong Witchita, me lie, me steal horse good as any, me big rascal, same as Witchita."

If an honest confession is good for the soul, this certainly was a case in point, if there is any truth in physiognomy, for a more cunning rascally countenance no one ever saw.

He rode off in company with some of the party when they left, having succeeded in getting a handkerchief and some other articles, either by begging or stealing.

Se-na-co and some of the chiefs, with their followers, left us during the day, shaking hands all round and apparently very friendly. They had dined and supped with us several times, behaving with great decorum, sitting at table and using knives and forks, but wild Indian-like, never stopping until every thing edible was consumed. This peculiarity applies, in a great measure, to all Indians; so much so, that rations had to be issued to our Delawares for three days only at a time, for just as like as not, they would consume the whole in one day. They have no idea of economy or of to-morrow, but let that take care of itself.

All are proverbially hospitable, both to strangers and acquaintances, never turning a hungry man away empty as long as a scrap to eat remains in camp, but they are wasteful and improvident.

August 23d.—But few articles could be obtained in barter from these Indians, as they were so scantily supplied even with essentials, but what they had and would part with, was readily taken up by different persons in the command, conspicuous among whom was a full blooded Choctaw, a teamster, whom we had hired when we passed through the nation, a shrewd fellow, who had provided himself with quite a stock of goods, and obtained a good supply of white buckskins, bows and arrows, &c., in exchange for vermilion, looking-glasses and calico.

In connection with this subject, I may remark, that the present system of trading with the prairie tribes has a great effect in checking all efforts of the government to prevent depredations upon the frontier settlements, and in this way, viz., a number of Delawares, Shawnees and Kickapoos, have for several years visited these tribes, with such articles as are most necessary to them, and which they will have at any cost, and have made large profits by the traffic. The articles they take are of small value, such as tobacco, paint, knives, beads, calico and wampum; and as the Indians have nothing of sufficient value to exchange for them, except horses and mules, they necessarily give them, and in large numbers. All these animals are obtained by marauding upon the frontier, and in proportion to the amount traded for, so is the corresponding amount of depredation.

A good plan to prevent this, would be an annual donation

18*

by the government of such articles as are supplied by the traders, with the understanding that this should continue so long as no forays were made, and thereby depreciating the value of these articles, would render the trading business no longer profitable.

The tribes are accustomed to exchange presents in their friendly intercourse with each other, and have no idea of friendship under any other form; they also value the strength of attachment by the amount of presents received, as an incident related by Captain Marcy will illustrate.

He once held a talk with a chief of one of the tribes, and told him that the President of the United States was their friend, and wished to live on terms of peace with them. The chief replied, that he was much astonished to hear this, for judging by the few trifling presents the Captain had given his people, he was of opinion that the "Big Captain" held them in but little estimation.

There is no doubt but that a small amount of money, annually expended in this way, would go far towards doing away entirely with the many and frequently bloody depredations of these people upon our poorly protected frontier.

August 24th.—The Indians continued to leave in parties of two or three, during the day, until all were gone except Ketum-e-see and the invalid, who seemed to be great friends.

Neither had any thing to say, but lounged around under the trees, evidently with some object in view, which greatly excited our curiosity, but the weather was so intensely hot, that we could take but little interest in any thing except the means of keeping cool.

Our larder had been most bountifully supplied for a few days past by a dragoon from Fort Belknap, who with a party, an escort to an invalid officer, had been spending a week with us, and discovered a colony of squirrels in a bottom on the opposite side of the Clear Fork. They were a large species, tawny on the belly and legs, and grey on the back, and so numerous that he shot fifty-five in four days, (going out for an hour at a time before the heat of the day,) which made into a stew were deliciously delicate and juicy.

August 25th.—Ke-tum-e-see disclosed his intention in remaining this morning. He walked up to the Quarter Master's tent, and demanded more beef and corn, but was peremptorily refused, told that he must not expect any more, and must now look out for himself. He walked off very angry, and soon we saw his wives bustling round, preparing him to leave.

Some of us went down to his bivouac, and found him seated, looking as black as a thunder cloud, and taking no notice of anything.

The invalid was at the same time made ready, and when his slave had saddled and led up his horse, the women lifted him on and fastened him with great difficulty, every movement of the poor wretch being made with a groan.

Ke-tum-e-see's horse was then saddled and led up by his wives, when he mounted, and led the way across the prairie, not deigning to turn his head or grunt out a good bye, and this was the last of the Camanches.

The knowing ones predicted trouble from this man, whom they said was revengeful and treacherous. We kept a good look out for him, however, and were constantly on the alert, as we had been during our stay in that wild spot.

August 26th.—The weather was still intensely hot—averaging one hundred and six degrees in the shade—and as the twenty-seventh was Sunday, the Captain determined to commence his survey on Monday, the twenty-eighth; the party was consequently busy all day in preparations, and those of us who had the opportunity, kept as quiet as possible, as the most discreet plan under such a sun.

I thought we had done with the Camanches, but was mistaken. Towards evening one made his appearance in the distance, and proved to be Naroni; but oh, how changed from the Naroni of the council-fire. Dressed in an old torn vest, breech-cloth and leggins, with a shabby straw hat upon his head, his buffalo tail, medallions and uniform laid aside, the little man looked smaller still, and miserably forlorn. He had shot two bucks, and came to barter the carcases for corn. Lounging around for a time, and finding no trade, he rode off, and we saw no more of him.

August 27th.—Sunday, intensely hot, and a general quiet reigning in our camp.

Shifting their homes so constantly as these Nomades of

the plains do, they are very careless of offal about camp, and in time of plenty this evil accumulates.

Our visitors left their temporary abode in a very disgusting state—half gnawed bones, and masses of cooked and raw flesh lying around, which soon, under the sun's intense rays, made us sensible of their locality.

As a sanitary measure, the Captain determined to break up our camp on the morrow, and move farther up the stream, and though we should miss the fine spring at this point, we should be nearer the land to be surveyed, which would be more convenient.

August 28th to September 4th.—Last night was one of great excitement in our camp. About midnight a general stampede of our horses took place, and as Ke-tum-e-see had left in such a bad humour, we concluded of course that the Indians had stolen them, but immediate pursuit being ordered, they were found in a ravine some miles off, much frightened, but supposed to have been by wolves, large packs of which had been prowling and howling around us every night during our stay.

We had scarcely got quiet again, when a mounted dragoon rode into camp, calling loudly for the captain, and exclaiming that his comrade had been murdered at the rancho a mile above us.

An officer, with the Doctor and a sufficient force, were sent up, when it appeared that the express rider from Fort Belknap to Fort Chadbourne, with a single dragoon as escort, had arrived at the rancho about two o'clock, A. M., and not wishing to disturb the inmates, were quietly tying up their mules to feed them, as was their custom at this place, when a young man, who was sleeping in the open air, being aroused, rushed to the house and shouted Indians. The man inside sprang out of bed, and seizing his gun, rushed to the door and fired two shots, both taking effect upon the poor soldier and mortally wounding him. He lingered insensible until eight, A. M., and died. Our carpenter made a rude coffin, and we buried him upon a hill side, along side of a dragoon who had been killed sometime before, by the Witchitas.

This incident shows how exciting is frontier life, and how constantly upon the alert the settlers must be against attack or surprise.

We moved camp six miles up the stream, on the same prairie and to a similiar spot to the one we left, though the water was not so good.

Major Neighbours returned to his home near San Antonio, and took with him Conner, the two Jacobs and Jack Hunter —the Shawnee. We parted with the Major with regret, his fund of anecdote of Indian life and customs, and his great experience on the frontier, imparted with so much affability and enthusiasm had wiled away many an hour in camp and on the march, and we missed him very much.

We remained at this point until the fourth of September, the surveying parties actively employed in running the lines and marking them, which was done by raising mounds at intervals of half a mile along the line.

Our mess was well supplied with wild turkeys, catfish and turtles, and a stream in the vicinity, a tributary of the Clear Fork, afforded fine sport to anglers, with a fish called here a trout, but which proved to be a species of bass, very game and rising readily to the fly.

The soil was very fertile and the country around rich in minerals, and affording a fine field for geologizing.

The rock was limestone, appearing on the south-west edge of the prairie piled up in layers of rectangular blocks, looking in the distance like a regularly built fortification.

CHAPTER XV.

CAMP ON THE CLEAR FORK TO CAMP ON THE LOWER BRAZOS.

Survey concluded.—Leave for Fort Belknap.—Description of country passed over.—Manner of designating Indian Camps by the Delawares.—Arrive at Fort Belknap.—Indian Council held.—Bear Head the interpreter.—Description of Fort Belknap—Lieut. Givens, a true sportsman.—Puma chase.— March to Caddo Village.—Description of the Village.—Jim Shaw and his family.—Grasses met with on our trip,—Finish the Survey.—Leave for home.

SEPTEMBER 4th to 10th.—The surveying parties having concluded their labours, we struck tents this morning and marched to Fort Belknap, where we camped for a short time to procure stores and prepare for future work in locating and surveying lands for the Caddos, Jonies, Ah-nan-da-kas, To-wac-ko-nies, Wichitas, and Ton-kah-was, who exist in this neighbourhood.

The country passed over abounded in game, and we passed many deserted hunting-camps. Our Delawares displaying the same sagacity, before observed upon, in designating the name of the tribe, the number, and even the lodge of the chief.

Being curious to know what signs indicated these facts, I asked one of them, when he gave me the following information, which may be of great service to travellers on the prairie, enabling them, when finding a deserted camp, to know the friendly from the hostile Indians ; and thus, should they be hostile, avoid them by marching in a different direction from their trail. The Camanches make their lodges by placing poles in the ground, in a circle, and tying the tops together, forming a frame work in a conical shape, which they cover with buffalo hides.

The Wichitas make their lodges in the same manner, but do not unite the poles at the top—leaving an opening for the smoke, which when covered forms the frustrum of a cone.

The Kickapoos place the poles in a circle, but instead of bringing them to a point at top, bend them so as to unite in an arch with those opposite, thus making the lodge round on top.

The Delawares and Shawnees carry tents, but leave the poles standing wherever they encamp.

The Cherokees have tents also, but build their fires different from the Delawares; they place the wood in the fire with the sticks parallel, and burn from one end, pushing it into the fire as it burns away; whereas the others place each stick pointing to the centre of the fire, like the spokes of a wheel.

We arrived at Fort Belknap on the seventh.

At a council held here, the Jonies and Ah-nan-dah-kas were represented by Jose Maria, the Caddos by Ti-nah, the Wichitas and Wacos by O-che-rash and Ack-a-quash, and the To-wac-ko-nies, by Utsiocks, Jose Maria—a fine looking man about sixty — was spokesman. His speech was in substance as follows !

" I know our Great Father has power to do with us as he pleases ; we have been driven from our homes several times by the whites, and all we want is a permanent location, where we

19

shall be free from further molestation. We prefer being near the whites, that we may be free from the depredations of the wild tribes.

"Heretofore we have had our enemies, the whites on one side, and the Camanches on the other, and of the two evils, we prefer the former, as they allow us to eat what we raise, whilst the Camanches take every thing, and if we are to be killed, we would much rather die with full bellies ; we would therefore prefer taking our chances on the Brazos, where we can be near the whites."

The captain told them that their Great Father would do everything to make them happy and comfortable, if they would accede to his wishes, settle upon these lands, and confine themselves to agriculture. They all expressed themselves ready and willing to do so, and parted on very friendly terms.

The interpreter at this council was *Bear Head*, a famous Delaware, employed by the Indian agent for these tribes as guide and interpreter. His American name was Jim Shaw. He had been adopted into the Caddo tribe, and become a chief among them. He was the finest specimen of the Indian I saw during the trip, about fifty years old, full six feet six in height, as straight as an arrow, with a sinewy, muscular frame, large head, high cheek bones, wide mouth, and eye like an eagle—his countenance indicative of the true friend and dangerous enemy.

Fort Belknap, one of the most distant posts on this frontier, is situated about a mile from the Brazos, upon an elevated, sandy plain, and though called Fort, is destitute of any sign of fortification. One or two substantial stone buildings have been erected, but the major part are in the style called *jacal*—huts built of logs stuck up on one end and roofed in with long prairie grass, the quarters scattered over a very extended surface, affording a fine drill ground in front.

It was surprising how much the taste and ingenuity of the officers stationed here had done to improve the few advantages they had, and as usual the most unbounded hospitality met us at their doors.

Major Steen of the 2d Dragoons commanded the post, and had a garrison of two companies of dragoons commanded by Messrs. Tree and Givins, and one company of infantry commanded by Major Paul, all in fine health and discipline, a great credit to the officers, considering the arduous duties so small a command must perform in such an exposed position.

Lieutenant Givins is an ardent sportsman, and by care and judgment has succeeded in raising the finest pack of hounds —thirty-five in number—on the continent, combining the strong scent of the fox-hound, with greater speed than usually found possessed by them, and the courage of the bull-terrier. This result he effects by retaining only the swiftest and healthiest, crossing the swift ones with those having a good nose, taking care to keep the blood pure, and always running his pack in company with a bull-terrier, whose example teaches them courage, and also chasing wolves, which developes that quality. The colors he retains are the blue, the yellow and the black—the blue being the swiftest, the yellow largest and strongest, and the black the most courageous. He presented us with the skin of a full grown Texas lion or Puma, six feet six from tip to tip, shot by himself, and very perfectly preserved and stuffed.

The chase and capture of this animal was very exciting.

Lieutenant Givins was chasing a jackass rabbit, (which on the high and open plains afford fine runs and excellent sport,) when his dogs opened upon this trail, and by their animation showed they were in pursuit of no ordinary animal. After a hot run for a mile they bayed at the foot of a post oak, in the crotch of which the lion was perched, looking as large as a mule, and displaying a formidable set of teeth and claws. While in this position he was shot through the body, and making a long leap escaped into a thicket from which he was soon routed by the dogs, and after a short run took to another tree, where he was shot through the shoulder, bringing him down, preventing him from climbing again, and allowing the dogs a chance to worry him.

The whole pack, together with the horsemen, now closed in, and just as he was in the act of crouching to spring, Lieutenant Givins shot him in the right eye, which finished him.

In the fight, one of the dogs had his skull broken in by a stroke of the lion's claws, and another had his leg torn open; but it was a right royal hunt, and a glorious triumph to the Lieutenant's skill and good training.

The puma resembles the African lion in ferocity and

strength, having been known to carry off a full-grown hog. It has a very ferocious appearance when in motion, crouches at the approach of an enemy, and bounds off with great swiftness. It is seldom found as far north as Fort Belknap.

At Fort Belknap we saw the boy who was so cruelly mangled by the Camanches when in company with Mrs. Wilson, an account of whose sufferings and escape was published in the news of the day, during the fall of 1853.

This boy had been scalped and left for dead, but reviving, managed to get into Fort Belknap, and, at the time we saw him, promised to recover entirely, a new cuticle having formed over his denuded scull, but an attack of dysentery carried him off after a few day's illness.

Though these officers bear with the most Spartan spirit their isolation and privations, and merge all other feelings in their zeal and devotion to their profession, gathering around them comforts and means for pursuits only to be acquired by highly refined and enlightened gentlemen, yet I would that some of our brawlers in Congress, and on the hustings, could visit these remote posts, and see a soldier's life in its true colours. A sense of shame and injustice would cause them to blush for past misrepresentations, and not only shut their mouths for the future, but open their eyes to the true light of merit in these devoted men   Their's is no carpet-knight service, but a stern reality, which, calling forth all the energies of their natures, tempers them with the Christian virtues of forbearance and philanthropy—forbearance towards their enemies at court; philanthropy for the dusky children of the plains, with whom they are brought daily in contact.

September 10th to 30th.—Having obtained the necessary supplies, we marched this morning at sunrise, and crossing the Brazos, encamped at noon about fifteen miles below Fort Belknap, where a selection had been made for the Indians of a fine body of land with plenty of wood and water. Near this point was a Caddo village of about one hundred and fifty lodges. These were constructed by erecting a frame-work of poles, placed in a circle in the ground, the tops united in an oval form, strongly bound with withes, and thatched with long grass. They were about twenty-five feet in diameter at the base and twenty feet high, making a very comfortable shelter, and looking in the distance like hay or grain stacks.

Each person had a bunk raised from the ground and covered with skins, as a couch, and the fire was built in the centre, the smoke escaping from the apex of the cone.

Our quondam acquaintance, Jim Shaw, came down and encamped near us, remaining during our stay.

Jim led a Gypsy life, with his wife and two children, living entirely in tents, but providing many comforts for them unknown or unthought of by other Indians.

I visited his camp several times, and was surprised to find some domestic appendages which I did not expect to see with them, moving as they did from place to place, viz., two cats and some barn-yard fowls.

He seemed very fond of his family, and anxious that his

children might go to school, and that he might soon be settled on the Reserve, and have his farm and permanent home. He had provided his wife with an excellent side saddle, and in her tent I saw a *musquito bar*, a luxury scarcely to be expected in an Indian camp.

Near our camp I found large quantities of the black mesquite grass, a very favourite grass with all who have tried it, and I collected a stock of the seed, which I trust may stand our climate, as from the avidity with which our animals eat it, I am sure it would be a great addition to our northern crops, either for pasture or fodder. It grows about as high as timothy, and has a head on it like wheat. The grasses met with are the white gramma, the blue gramma, three varieties of the sedge, the buffalo grass, the bearded mesquite and the black mesquite.

Of these, the buffalo grass would make a beautiful sod for lawns, as its growth is very short and velvety, appearing more like the thickest kind of moss than grass. I observed that our horses eat it in preference to any other, even when it was quite dry, and green succulent grass in its vicinity. I could not procure any seed.

But few of the Indians came in to our camp, and those that did were some of the chiefs named, and a few war captains. Those we saw were not as fine looking nor as wild as the Camanches, but very subdued and demure in their appearance and demeanor.

The tract to be surveyed was located on both sides of the

Brazos, which here was very crooked, the water very bitter, and the bed of stream quicksand. The amount to be surveyed, twelve square leagues, took of course a much longer time than on the Clear Fork, added to which was a difference in the kind of ground, a portion of this being quite mountainous. The surveying party worked diligently, however, and by the twenty-ninth had completed their labours, and on the thirtieth, we struck tents and started on our homeward trip by way of Fort Belknap.

CHAPTER XVI.

THE INDIANS OF THE COUNTRY.

Names of the tribes.—John Conner, the Delaware Guide.—Customs among the Delawares.—Traits of character with anecdotes illustrative.—Description of other tribes.—Creek green corn dance and feast.—Traditions among the tribes.—Incident of the Quapaws.—The Camanches.—Number and division.—Supposed origin.—Religious ideas.—Contempt for the whites.—Treatment of women.—Customs among them.—Their habits.—Anecdotes of the Camanches.—General remarks.

THE Indians who subsist in the vast regions of the far South-west, are the Camanches, Wacos, Caddos, Jonies, Ahnan-dah-kas, To-wac-co-nies, Ton-kah-ways, Paluxsies, Moscalara, Apaches, Lipans, Kechies, Witchitas, Kickapoos, Quapaws, Kioways, and Navajoes, all Nomadic and the Creeks, Seminoles, Choctaws, Chickasaws, Shawnees, and Delawares, who live in permanent homes.

The principal settlement of the Delawares is on Caw river, Missouri, but there is quite a number settled at old Fort Arbuckle, in the Choctaw nation, from whence our hunters and guides were procured.

John Conner, our quondam interpreter and guide, was a very intelligent man, differing from the generality of Indians in this respect, viz., he would not only give a direct answer to a question, but also express a decided opinion and support it by argument.

As a general thing, Indians are non-committal, their eternal "may be so," always giving them a hole to escape by.

From Conner, I learned a great deal about his tribe. The Delawares are by far the most intelligent Indians in the South-west. By a law of their tribe, a wife is sole owner of all the property she may be possessed of at the time of her marriage, and all she may afterwards accumulate. The practice of purchasing a wife still exists among them. Polygamy is also allowed, but is by no means common.

Conner told me that the price of a wife was "one horse, five blankets, and goods so high," holding his hand about a foot from the ground, a very indefinite quantity to be sure, but of course understood to mean enough to satisfy the parent. When the bargain is concluded the woman must accede, there is no alternative, and hence much misery is entailed upon families, feelings of dislike having carried individuals so far as to cause them to commit murder.

The bashful youths, get their mothers to make the bargain for them, and Jackson, who had quarreled with his wife before leaving home—amused me very much by his description of how he intended to get another when he returned.—He said, "my wife all the time mad, me go out hunt, come back, he say, where you been devil; all time mad, den me say may be so you quit, den he go, now go home, plenty of money, may be so my mudder he catch nudder wife," throwing his arm out with the same motion he used when throwing the lariat to noose his horse.

The Delawares are shrewd and fond of money, but only as a means of gratification of either appetite or fancy, never saving up any thing for the future. Stealing horses seems to be a vice and propensity peculiar to all Indians, and the Delawares are not an exception. Like all Indians, the labour of planting corn, taking care of stock and all drudgery is performed by their women.

They are very inquisitive but not credulous. Captain Marcy once showed a Delaware a pocket compass. He was much interested, watched the oscillations of the needle and the effect of passing a piece of steel over the glass, then walked away keeping his eyes attentively fixed upon the needle and the invariable manner in which it settled down to the same spot. He could not understand it, but with Indian incredulity, remarked, " May be so he lie sometime."

The Captain, upon another occasion, endeavoured to explain to one of them the magnetic telegraph, and told him that by means of it a message could be sent one thousand miles, and an answer returned in ten minutes. He seemed much interested, but made no remark until the Captain told him to explain it to a Camanche who was standing by. He replied, "Captain me, not tell him dat ; me not believe it meself."

Although reliable, when pledged to perform any duty, they are like all Indians, tricky.

Captain Black Beaver—who has been mentioned before, and who lives at old Fort Arbuckle—had been frequently in the employ of the government, and out with the officer who relates this anecdote, but declining to go upon a late expedition, he procured for the officer the services of John Bushman, another Deleware.

The officer told Bushman to inform his corps of hunters and guides that they would be paid one dollar and a half a day and one ration. Shortly after this, it was necessary to have an interpreter to a wild tribe that was met, and Bushman acted.

After the talk he said to the officer, " You not tell me what you give me." The officer insisted that he had told him one dollar and a half per day. He replied " Black Beaver he say two dollar half one day." The officer told him that he made his own bargains, and the government had no money to squander, but that on condition of his acting as interpreter he would increase his pay half a dollar.

On the return of the expedition, and after he was paid, the officer asked him, " John, will you go again?" " No," was his reply, " dat government he not got no money." It turned out to be a plan of Black Beaver to share half of the two dollars and a half, but did not succeed.

They are brave to a fault, never turning their backs upon the foe. The following anecdote, related of this same Captain Black Beaver, is an illustration :

He accompanied a government expedition, some years since, into the Camanche country, and being out upon a scout one day, accompanied by a white man attached to the train, they were suddenly surprised by seven Camanches, who, circling round them, made every hostile demonstration.

The white man, being mounted upon a fleet blood mare, proposed to run for camp, when Beaver turned to him, and cocking his rifle, said, very quietly, "May be so you run, may be so I shoot you." He continued his determined manner towards the Camanches, and the consequence was himself and companion returned safely to the train

They are very proud of their race, and nothing insults them more than to be called out of the name of Indian. An officer was sent off with a detachment of our party, and took Jackson as hunter and guide. To our surprise, the Indian returned alone, looking very sour and angry. He said, "Dat man he say you dog, you no hunt deer. Me no dog, me Indian; me not can kill deer, me not see him close. Me kill deer, me see him. Me not stay, me not dog, me Indian," raising himself proudly to his full height and striking his hand forcibly upon his breast. At heart they hate the white man, but are shrewd enough to know that it is for their interest to be friendly and faithful.

Their extraordinary powers of endurance and perseverance have been frequently tested. An officer once ordered one of them to follow a trail and see where it led to. He returned shortly and said it led off into the prairie and to no particular spot. He was told this was not satisfactory and must follow it up and find out certainly. He left immediately and for weeks nothing was heard of him, when no sooner had

20

the command arrived at the first settlement than he made his appearance, and told the officer that the trail he ordered him to follow, terminated there, having with indomitable perseverance followed it several hundred miles through that wild country, subsisting upon what he could kill, but determined to obey orders to the letter.

Their sagacity in detecting and describing signs in the prairie I have before remarked upon, and it appears to be intuitive and peculiar to the Indian. In crossing a trail one day, one of them picked up a blade of grass that had been crushed, and said that the trail was two days old, when to all appearance it was perfectly fresh; subsequent events proved he was correct. At another time, the attention of one of them was called to some tracks in the sand, looking like the impression made by the toes, foot and heel of a bear, he immediately pointed to some blades of grass hanging about ten inches over the marks, and explained that when the wind blew, the blades were pressed over, and their oscillations scooped out the light sand in the form seen.

These traits, besides their wonderful powers of judging of country and knowledge of Indian character and habits, render them invaluable on the frontier, and it would be well for the government to attach a few to each company of troops engaged in this service, thus enabling them to operate to much greater advantage against the prairie tribes.

The Shawnees live on Little River, a tributary of the Canadian. They assimilate to the Delawares, and intermarry with them, the same traits of character being observ able.

The Seminoles (under Wild Cat, of Florida-war memory) live on the Rio Grande. The Choctaws and Chickasaws have been already described, and the Creeks live on a Reserve bounded on the north by the south shore of the Arkansas.

Conner described to me the Creek green corn dance and feast, which he said is a religious ceremony with them. As soon as the corn is edible, the different villages assemble, and after some preliminary ceremonies, begin to swallow large quantities of a decoction of a species of lobelia, called among them the " *Devil's shoe-string.*'" This brings on violent vomiting and purging, until the whole stomach and bowels are cleansed, when they proceed to gorge themselves with green corn to satiety, and the quantity consumed is according to him enormous. They then sleep, and afterwards commence the green corn dance, which lasts until all are worn down with fatigue; a singular custom and one scarcely to be imagined even among savages.

These six tribes all live in houses, and cultivate the soil to a greater or less extent, in a majority of cases barely sufficiently so for a support.

The Caddos, Ionies and Ah-nan-dah-kas, numbered about seven hundred and fifty warriors, women and children ; speak the same language and intermarry. They have a tradition that they issued from the hot springs of Arkansas, and from that went to Red River near Natchitoches, and finally to the Brazos.

Of the To-wac-o-nies there were fifty-one men, sixty-three women and fifty-five children.

The Wacos numbered sixty-five men, eighty-eight women, and seventy-two children.

These five tribes were living in great harmony, had nume-rous herds of horses and mules, all stolen from the whites, and at some of their temporary straw villages raised corn, beans, squashes and melons. They were all of pure Indian blood, and though their women were said to be far from chaste, they did not mingle with white men.

As far as could be ascertained, there were eighty Witchita men, one hundred and twelve women, and one hundred and twenty-two children.

They are most arrant horse thieves and scoundrels, and have given more trouble to the settlers in Texas than any other tribe. They have a village upon Rush Creek, a tribu-tary to the Washita, a kind of rendezvous for them, from which they make constant marauding expeditions.

The Kickapoos live on the Washita near Fort Arbuckle; are very famous hunters, and somewhat less savage, though with ardent propensities for horse-stealing. The Paluxsies are but a mere remnant, wandering from place to place in a destitute and squalid condition. They number about sixty as a maximum. The Tonkaways have a tradition that their progenitor came into the world by the agency of a wolf, and commemorate the event by the wolf dance.

This dance is conducted with the greatest secrecy, and it is only by the most urgent solicitation that spectators are admitted to this curious scene.

Upon entering the dance lodge—a long, low building made of poles and thatched with grass—about fifty performers were observed, all dressed in wolf skins, so as perfectly to represent the animal. They went around on all fours, howled and made other demonstrations peculiar to the wolf. After going around awhile they all stopped, and one smelled the earth at a particular spot, howled and began to scratch. A general scratching then took place, and pretty soon they unearthed a genuine live Tonkaway, who had been interred for the purpose. As soon as he was dragged out a general council was held, when the Tonkaway addressed them thus, "You have brought me into the world and I know not what to do for a subsistence; it would have been better to let me remain as I was. I shall starve in this world." After mature deliberation they put a bow and arrows into his hands and told him he must do as the wolves do, rob, kill and wander from place to place, and never cultivate the soil, and this they have done ever since.

The Apaches and Lipans are very numerous, fierce and warlike. They are more generally supplied with fire-arms than other tribes, and are in a state of constant hostility to the whites.

The Kechies numbered about one hundred warriors, and the Quapaws only thirty-five.

All these tribes use the horse in war and in the chase, supply themselves with both horses and mules by stealing, and always have a good supply.

The Quapaws, a small remnant of the once powerful Arkansas, are an illustration of the rapid degeneracy and necessarily final disappearance of the Indian. Once called by way of distinction "the fine men," and complimented as the most distinguished warriors, for having conquered the powerful Chickasaws, at the time the most numerous and warlike among the tribes, they are now reduced to a handful of squalid half starved beggars, soon to be lost entirely or merged in some other tribe.

An incident is related of one of their encounters with the Chickasaws, which shows the once great magnanimity of a nation now so near annihilation.

The Chickasaw chief thought most prudent to make a precipitate retreat in consequence of having no powder, which when told to the Quapaw chief, he determined that they should be put upon an equality with his band, and ordering all his warriors to empty their powder horns into a blanket, made an equal division and sent one-half to his enemies; the fight began, and ended in a signal defeat of the Chickasaws.

The Camanches and Kioways are the most numerous tribes in the South West, have similar habits, but do not speak the same language—nor do the Kioways roam as far south as the Camanches.

The Camanches are the "lords of the plains." They are the most warlike and powerful, and number over twenty thousand. They are separated into three grand divisions; the Northern, Middle and Southern, and these sub-divided into bands commanded by separate chiefs. They suppose that their forefathers came from a country towards the setting sun. They acknowledge a supreme ruler and director, whom they call the Great Spirit; but in their devotions appeal directly to the sun and earth, saying that one is the great cause of life, and the other the receptacle and producer of all that sustains life; accordingly when they eat or drink, they sacrifice a good portion to the Great Spirit, saying that otherwise he would be angry, and bring upon them ill-fortune. They say that they cannot worship God, he is too far off, but they can worship the sun, who is between them and the Supreme Being. They entertain an inherent dislike for the whites and are very suspicions of their motives in visiting them. Some of their chiefs have visited Washington, and returned with strong impressions of the strength of the whites, but the most of them believe the Camanches to be the most powerful nation in existence, and any opposition to this idea only subjects the relator to ridicule and want of confidence. Captain Marcy relates a conversation he overheard between a Camanche and a Delaware, in which the latter endeavoured to prove to the Camanche that the earth was round, and that it revolved round the sun. The Camanche indignantly asked if he took him for an idiot, that any man could see that the earth was perfectly level by only looking off, over the prairie, and moreover his grandfather had been to the west end of it, where the sun went down behind a wall. The Delaware continued to describe to him other things he had seen among the whites, all of which the Camanche attributed to some necromancy or spell put upon him by them, and only deigned to reply, by repeating "Hush, you fool."

An intelligent Chickasaw once visited them and endeavoured to impress upon one of them the benefits that would result to them if they would cease their wandering life, and learn to read, write and cultivate the soil; that the whites had taught his people and they had become a happy people. The Camanche replied that he would willingly agree to be taught, but that *the whites were such great rascals* he could not trust them, nor consent to be taught by them; that if the Choctaws and Chickasaws would send out men to teach them, they would excuse those wishing to learn from war and hunting, but that he must think there were very few, if any, *honest* white men; showing that he entertained bitter hostility towards us.

The Camanche men are of middle stature, light copper-colored complexions, and intelligent countenances, but the women are short, crooked-legged, and far from good-looking. The men are grossly licentious, treating female captives in a most cruel and barbarous manner; but they enforce rigid chastity upon their women, every dereliction from which is punished by cutting off the tip of the nose, as an indelible mark of shame. Their women are looked upon as slaves and beasts of burden, and every degrading service that can be inflicted upon them falls to their lot, yet strange to say they seem contented, and submit without a murmur. They are not prolific, a woman seldom having more than three children, which if males, are nurtured with great care, whilst the females are abused and often beaten unmercifully.

When a man wants a wife, he goes to the head of the family (who, according to their laws, is either the father, or if he is dead, the son who has most distinguished himself in war or hunting, even if he should be a younger son) and lays down before him such goods as he thinks will be acceptable, and then sits down at some distance to await the result. After smoking a pipe, the goods are examined, and if acceptable, the girl is led out and handed over. For her there is no alternative, and repugnance often occasions " liasons" with former lovers.

Should an elopement take place, in such cases the husband and his friends follow until they overtake the fugitives, when formerly the man was put to death, but now they compromise by purchase, the husband takes horses until he is satisfied, the wife remains the property of her choice, and all return to the village contented.

The old men get possession of all the young girls they can, and make a profit out of them in this way, viz : a young man will pay a large bonus to be admitted as a member of the family and allowed to marry, after which, besides the bonus, part of all that he obtains in war or hunting, becomes the property of the old head of the family; they often liberate prisoners on the same conditions.

Young girls are not reluctant to marry very old men, if they are chiefs, being sure of always having something to eat, if there is anything in camp, the chief always having first choice.

A shrewd trick related of Mo-ko-cho-pee—a deceased chief of the Southern Camanches—amused me very much. The old fellow was one of a party that visited Washington, and was much interested with what he saw, and wished to travel generally through the States, but finding this required money, he returned to his tribe determined to accumulate sufficient to pay his expenses on the grand tour. Whenever any of his band—which they often did, after returning from a foray, would bring him coins to ask the value, he would always tell them it was best to throw them away, as they were worthless; knowing they would follow his advice, he would watch closely where the coins were thrown, and going out secretly, secure them. In this way, it was found when he died, that he had accumulated a very large sum of money.

In trading they are careful to have a good price fixed for a herd of horses and mules, by displaying the best stock first, when all the rest are expected to be taken at the same price. They also prefer a variety rather than quantity, even though the goods may not be so valuable.

They never travel twice upon the same trail, and on leaving

a camp, separate into small parties, each one taking a different route, and arriving at some appointed place. They eat
nothing but meat, and are called among the other tribes
" the buffalo eaters."

Always travelling upon an empty stomach, they ride fast
and far, then eat enormously, and afterwards sleep immediately, when they are again ready for the road.

No young man is admitted into the ranks of the braves
until he has stolen a number of horses and mules and taken
scalps, the consequence is that parties will go off and begone
sometimes two years, and it is these who commit the most
horrid atrocities upon the plains.

They require no equipments on these expeditions but their
horses and weapons, subsisting upon what they find on their
route.

When a chief wishes to go to war, he mounts on horseback, holding erect a long pole with a red flag tipped with
eagle's feathers attached, and rides through the camp singing
his war-song. Those who wish to go fall in, and after going
round for a while they dismount, and the war-dance commences. This routine is gone through with several days,
until sufficient volunteers are collected. Each warrior
provides his own horse and equipments, and they manage to
mount themselves upon white or cream-colored horses if
possible, which they paint all over in the most fantastic
figures imaginable.

The whole thing is voluntary, but one who behaves

cowardly is disgraced, nor do they return until the wish to do so is unanimous. Should the expedition prove unsuccessful they separate into small parties, and on their way back to their tribe, rob and kill whenever an opportunity offers, as it is considered disgraceful to return empty handed; they also shave their horses' tails and put on mourning for a long time. If it is successful, they send a herald ahead to announce their arrival, when great preparations are made to receive them, the old women set up a shout of exultation when they appear, the scalp dance commences, and is performed with all the ceremonies.

When a Camanche warrior dies, he is buried upon the top of the highest hill near camp, with his face to the East, his war-horse is killed and his weapons burnt up, his other animals having their manes and tails shaved close, and the women have to cut their hair close, as a symbol of mourning. For a long time after the decease the relatives and friends assemble morning and evening to cry, and howl and cut themselves with knives. This ceremony takes place outside the encampment, and lasts sometimes a month. They bury immediately after death, not permitting the body to remain above ground any longer than necessary to prepare the grave.

When a young warrior dies, they mourn a long time, but when an old person dies, they mourn but little, saying that they cannot live forever, and it was time they should go.

They believe all go up to a place above, where they are

happy, that they are permitted to visit the earth at night, but must return at daylight.

The Osages and other northern tribes have the same custom of howling at the death of friends, with this addition, that presents are distributed to the mourners ; many therefore come to howl in expectation of getting a present.

Jim Shaw told me that he knew one old woman who kept up howling so long, that one of the friends of the deceased asked her what she wanted, and what she howled for, she immediately said for a horse, which was given her, and she became silent. He also told me that the practice of cutting themselves, was done in many instances in order to promote tears by the pain.

The Caddos howl when in want and distress, saying that the Great Spirit will hear and assist them if they cry to him, —an untutored and primitive idea of prayer.

Whilst Major Neighbours was with the Tonkaways, a band of forty Camanches, headed by Mo-ko-cho-pee, came into camp, and were very exacting in their demands, ordering the Tonkaways to take care of their horses, and get them some supper, which was immediately done, and at the same time forty of their best looking girls were assigned to their guests. The Major endeavored to get on good terms with the chief, told him he was Indian agent for Texas, and that the people of that State desired to keep peace with all the Indians, and especially with the Camanches.

The chief replied, that the whites were great rascals, but

21

he believed the Major to be a very clever fellow, and he particularly admired the coat he wore, whereupon the Major pulled it off and gave it to him. Another then admired his vest, another his pantaloons, another his boots, and so on to his cravat and stockings, thus completely denuding the Major of a new outfit he had made in Washington, and leaving him in his shirt. He says, however, that naked though he was, he laughed heartily at the grotesque appearance of these fellows, strutting about, each with some portion of his wardrobe upon his tawny figure. They were so much pleased with his generosity, that they insisted upon his going along with them, and told him that if he would join their horse-stealing expedition, they would adopt him into their tribe,—thinking he might prevent them from depredating, he went with them. A few days afterwards, they came to the rancho of an old Mexican, where the Major applied for some beef for them, telling the Mexican that he would see him paid ; the old man refused unless the money was paid beforehand, when the chief told him that he wanted two beeves, and if they were not forthcoming in half an hour, he would burn his rancho and kill his stock, it is needless to say the beeves were handed over. The Major remained a few days longer with them, but getting tired persuaded them to let him go. This anecdote illustrates how completely the Camanches have ruled in the plains, the terror of the other wandering tribes, and the scourge of the frontier settlements, their reign it is to be hoped is at an end.

In roaming over the plains of the South-west I was struck with their similarity to the steppes of Tartary and the deserts of Arabia, but not more so than with the resemblance of the inhabitants of both.

The Nomades of the old world and the wild Indian of the prairie have no permanent abiding place, but where their lodges are pitched there are their homes. Their respective governments are patriarchal, sanctioned by the masses, and guided by the counsels of the elders. They never cultivate the soil, but subsist upon plunder and the chase. They are alike in their attachment to the horse and expertness in horsemanship. Coinciding in their views of the rights of property, they consider stealing from strangers as perfectly legitimate, are the greatest marauders on earth, and he who is most expert and successful is the greatest among them.

In minor and domestic customs they are identical. Polygamy is allowed, they sit cross-legged upon mats, are very fond of tobacco, and saddle, bridle, and mount their horses from the right side, they also eat with their fingers.

The estimation in which a successful robber is held, is illustrated by an anecdote of an old chief, who said he had four sons who were a great comfort to him in his declining years, as they could steal more horses than any young men in the tribe.

The favourite horse of the wild Indian is his constant companion, and it is when mounted and going through with his war-exercises that he shows to the best advantage. In the saddle from boyhood to old age, he acquires such skill and dexterity as to realize the appearance of the famed Centaur of mythology. Throwing himself entirely on one side of his horse, he will discharge his arrows with the utmost rapidity from beneath the animal's neck, whilst at full speed, shielding his person by the animal's body, and regaining his seat with no effort except the muscles of the leg.

The bow is their favourite weapon, and being placed in the hands of the boys at an early age, they acquire extraordinary proficiency, rendering them not only successful in the chase but formidable in war. At short distances, they will frequently throw an arrow entirely through the huge carcass of the buffalo.

With a shield made of untanned buffalo-hide, they protect themselves from this weapon in war, fastening it upon the left arm, so as not to interfere with the free use of the hand, and performing their feats of horsemanship; equipped in this way, with the addition of a war-club, made of a heavy stone, grooved in around the centre to receive a withe bound with buffalo-hide.

Brave to a fault, they always fight in the open prairie, charging boldly up to their enemies, discharging their missiles and advancing and retreating with great rapidity.

Though kind and hospitable to strangers, and fraternal in their intercourse with each other, they are implacable in their hatred, and any insult offered can only be atoned for by blood.

They believe in amulets and charms, and in dreams—the

vapour-bath is used both for healing diseases and as a preparation for young men who wish to assume the rank of warriors.

They have no idea of Christianity, nor have missionaries ever visited them, offering a wide field for those philanthropists who are now sending the blessings of the gospel to distant lands : here is a people at our very doors, to whom we may atone in this way, in some measure, for the wrongs they have suffered at our hands.

Their present and former modes of subsistence being rapidly on the decline, it becomes an interesting question what is to become of these people. The views of the government, in this expedition, would ameliorate their condition, but their inherent dislike of the white man and his customs, are the great barrier to its success, and of three extremities my opinion is, they will adhere to their present life, and finally disappear entirely—they must either work, steal, or starve ; stealing being more congenial, they will continue to follow it until repeated chastisement accomplishes their destruction.

CONCLUSION.

October 1st.—We were now about to separate, the excitement of the trip was over; the object of the expedition was attained, and we were all heartily tired and anxious once more for the comforts of home and the society of friends.

We had been fortunate in not losing a man by sickness or casualty, and in this respect had great cause for congratulation after the great privations suffered, and the extent of country passed over.

Leaving the train in charge of the subalterns to march to Fort Arbuckle, the Captain, Doctor, and myself, passed rapidly over the road to Fort Smith, where we arrived on the fifteenth, when the Captain and myself procured a conveyance by land through Arkansas and Missouri, and arriving at Jefferson City on the twenty-fourth, the first of November found us both at our respective homes, after a six months absence, and thus ended my tour on the Prairies.